family walks *in* scotland

compiled by **Colin Hogarth** in association with **walkscotland.com**

THE IN PINN®

is an imprint of

Neil Wilson Publishing Ltd
303 The Pentagon Centre
36 Washington Street
GLASGOW
G3 8AZ

Tel: 0141 221 1117
Fax: 0141 221 5363
E-mail: info@nwp.co.uk
www.nwp.co.uk
www.theinpinn.co.uk

Walk route text and photography © James Carron,
Colin Hogarth and Andrew Jarret 2002
Reprinted 2004

Maps by Barbara Hogarth
Designed by Belstane

ISBN 1 903238 58 7

Typeset in Bosis and New Caledonia
Printed in Poland

Contents

Contents

(continued)

Introduction

Launched on to the World Wide Web in September 1999, walkscotland.com has become one of the leading outdoor sites in the country and one of Scotland's best hillwalking resources.

We have an archive containing well over 200 routes, with new ones being added every week. Our walks range in length from short evening strolls to more adventurous multi-day backpacking trips.

We've teamed up with the In Pinn to bring you a collection of our favourite 100 family walks in Scotland. They are spread across the country, from Dumfries and Galloway in the south, to Caithness in the north, and from Angus in the east to the Isle of Skye in the west, so you shouldn't have to travel far for a great day out.

In addition to a step-by-step guide to each route, a fact file, map and photographs, every walk in this book has an address which will direct you to that route on the website. This allows you to link directly to **walkscotland.com** where you can download a free route card for each walk, find additional photos and maps, receive updates and access plenty of other useful information. After selecting a walk in the book, simply download and print the route card and take that with you.

We hope to inspire you to get out and explore the wonders of Scotland's magnificent countryside. There's plenty to see and do and the routes we've selected cover a wealth of terrain and scenery, from bracing coastal hikes to treks into more remote glens flanked by spectacular mountains.

Before you go . . .

To ensure you get the most from your hike it's worth taking a few sensible precautions before you venture out. Here are some tips to help you make the most of your walking.

Plan ahead

Before you go you should always select a route that is within the capabilities of everyone in your family, or group, and refer to the relevant maps so you get a good idea of what to expect.

All the routes in this book have been graded to help you choose a suitable walk. With 100 walks, spread across the country, there are plenty of options, whether you want a short stroll or a more energetic hike. You can also adapt the walks to suit what you want to do, and get what you want out of it.

Be well equipped

The Scottish weather can be very unpredictable, so go well prepared, even on low-level routes. In summer a good fleece and lightweight waterproof outer jacket should be sufficient but for winter invest in thermal underwear, the best wind and water resistant jacket you can afford, and always take along a hat and gloves. In summer, a wide-brimmed hat is a good idea, as is suntan lotion, particularly for children. On shorter walks the sort of clothing your kids wear to play outdoors should be fine. But take along an extra sweatshirt, just in case they feel cold. And don't forget a waterproof jacket. Leave spare clothes in the car so they can change at the end of the walk. If they enjoy walking and you go out regularly, then you may want to invest in specialist outdoor clothing for children. Regatta, Wynnster and Togz all have kid's ranges, while Bodge the Badger has great stuff for youngsters. Helly Hansen do thermal base layers for children that will keep them snug in colder weather. Having a baby or toddler shouldn't mean you can't go walking. Special carriers are available from outdoor shops – just make sure the little one is wrapped up well, and that you keep checking up on them.

Proper footwear is of paramount importance all year round and again a good pair of boots, correctly fitted and broken in, will keep feet dry, warm and comfortable and help you avoid blisters which can ruin any walk.

For short walks, children should be fine in trainers or welly boots. On longer routes, a proper pair of walking boots is recommended and these are available in children's size – pop along to your local outdoor shop and see what's on offer.

Whatever they wear on their feet, make sure your kids have good thick socks on – at least two pairs – to prevent rubbing and blisters, and above all make sure whatever they are wearing on their feet fits properly.

Remember to take an up-to-date Ordnance Survey or Harvey's map (where available) covering your route, plus a compass, whistle, torch, spare food and a survival bag. The latter item is a large plastic sack, usually bright orange, which is big enough to accomodate an adult . It can be a lifesaver in the event of an accident, providing a casualty with protection from the elements. Survival bags cost just a few pounds at outdoor shops and every walker should carry one in their rucksack.

Food and drink

Food and drink may seem obvious requirements but you would be surprised at how many people don't carry enough when venturing out into the wilds. Constant exercise burns off plenty of calories and you need to replenish these. The best advice is to eat small amounts, often. Pack sandwiches, pork pies or sausage rolls and things like fruit, chocolate, cereal bars, nuts, dried fruit and mint cake. Include your childen's favourite snacks and juice to keep them happy and take sweets or chocolate to keep the young walkers motivated and to award effort.

Fluid intake is vital. While streams are plentiful in the great outdoors, it may not always be safe to drink from them so carry your own. If you do take water from a stream, only do so on high ground and ensure the point where you take it is fast-flowing and away from potential sources of pollution. Avoid taking water from streams running through agricultural land and coniferous forestry.

Know how to use a map and compass

While the routes contained within this book are straightforward and easy to follow, it's always worth learning how to use a map and compass, particularly if you plan to do a lot of walking. These are skills that take very little time to master and being proficient allows you to become more adventurous in your own route planning and to appreciate your surroundings more while out.

Understanding maps

At first glance, a map can look pretty complicated. However, it is simply a picture of the ground, viewed from above. The first thing you'll probably notice are the brown contour lines. If the world was completely flat, there would be no need for them. But, as it isn't, cartographers devised contour lines to show all the ups and downs. Contour lines join places of equal height and enable you to interpret the shape of the ground. Where they are close together, the slope is steep and when they are further apart, it is more gentle. Equally spaced contour indicate a straight slope, while, on a concave slope, the lines are more closely spaced at the top. On a convex slope, the lines are closer together at the bottom.

All maps come with a key or legend that explains the lines, colours or symbols used to indicate features, such as roads, rivers, forestry, buildings and bridges and studying this first will unravel a lot of the mystery.

One important feature of maps is the grid lines, a network of vertical and horizontal lines. These are blue on Ordnance Survey Landrangers and black on Harvey's maps. The grid lines each have grid numbers and these can be used to accurately pinpoint a specific location on a map, known as a grid reference (GR). The vertical lines are called 'eastings' while the horizontal ones are called 'northings'. The corresponding grid numbers are printed along the top and bottom of the map for the eastings and up and down either side of the map for the northings. The OS also print them at intervals across the Landranger sheets.

Throughout this book grid references are given for the starting point of a route. To use these you will have to know how to read a six-figure grid number. The first two digits in the grid number relate to the easting. Go along the bottom of the map to find the corresponding two-digit number. The fourth and fifth digits are the northing. Look up the side of the map to find this two-digit number. Now, go up the vertical easting line and across the horizontal northing line to the point where the two lines meet.

To the right of the easting line and above the northing line you have a grid square measuring two centimetres on either side and representing 1km square on the ground. The location you want is within this square and to narrow it down precisely, you have to use the third and sixth digit in your six-figure grid reference.

A small ruler can assist at this point and most compasses also have a measuring device along one edge to assist. Divide the square with 10 vertical and 10 horizontal lines, each spaced 2mm apart. Take the third digit from your grid reference and from the vertical easting line on the left of the square, move to the right across the square to the corresponding vertical line. If the number is '6', for instance, you will move 12mm across the grid square. Next, take the sixth digit of the grid number and repeat the process, this time starting from the horizontal line across the bottom of the square and moving up. Where the two lines meet, you have your location. As an example, if the third and sixth digits

are both '5', the location you are looking for is right in the centre of the grid square. If the third digit is '1' and the sixth digit '9', the spot is right up in the top left hand corner of the square.

Through regular use, the process of giving or locating a grid reference becomes very simple and most walkers work out the location they want by estimating where the tenths fall in the square.

If you get into difficulties in the countryside and need to summon assistance, being able to work out the grid reference of where a casualty is and then passing it on to rescuers saves a lot of time and uncertainty.

Grid lines can also be used when estimating distance. The lines are spaced to represent 1km on the ground so, for example, if you are following a track running due east, each time you 'pass through' a grid line, you have walked 1km. You can also chart your progress on a map by identifying features as you pass them.

Take a course

If you're new to hillwalking, it's worth getting advice from people in the know before you set out. If you've friends or relatives who go walking, have a chat with them, or accompany them on one of their trips.

Another idea is to sign up on a course or evening class. The outdoor education departments of local authorities often run these, as do some colleges. The Mountaineering Council of Scotland (MCofS) organise safety and training courses covering subjects like mountain first aid, navigation and winter safety.

Finally, if you enjoy walking but feel more comfortable in the company of a group, consider joining a walking club. The MCofS holds a list of these, with contact details.

Leave written word of your intended route

When you head into the countryside, it's a sensible precaution to leave word of where you are going with someone before you set off, just in case you do get into any difficulties. Filling in a Route Card is a good idea. This contains details of your route, the number of people in your group and other important information that could assist the police and rescuers if you fail to return. You can download one at **www.walkscotland.com/routecard.htm**. Once you've completed the various parts of the card, leave it with a responsible person – a friend, relative or neighbour, at your B&B, with a hostel warden or hotel receptionist. Make sure you contact them immediately upon your return to let them know you are back safely.

First aid

One area where advanced preparation can really pay off is in knowing simple first aid. You should always take a small first aid kit with you, just in case. Most of the time it will remain tucked away at the bottom of your rucksack, but it's better to be safe than sorry. You can either make one up with items from the medicine cabinet at home, or buy one for around £10 from a chemist or outdoor shop. It should contain some plasters (for cuts and scrapes), a crepe bandage (for twists or sprains), antiseptic cream or wipes (for cleaning wounds), painkillers (such as paracetamol) and a small pair of scissors. You may want to include a selection of other dressings, anti-histamine cream and midge repellent. Keep a close eye on kids to make sure they don't end up covered in cuts or grazes and have a supply of treats close at hand to cheer them up if they do.

Blisters

Blisters plague many hillwalkers. They can turn a pleasant trek into an agonising ordeal. Caused by friction, repeated pressure to skin areas, or extremes in temperature, either hot or cold, blisters are fluid filled sacks with a thin layer of almost transparent skin over them.

Fortunately, they can be treated with relative ease. The priority is to keep the area of the blister clean, to prevent infection. As a general rule blisters should not be broken, unless they are very painful, or in an area where there is continued boot pressure, which will break the blister with continued walking. As long as the blister is left intact, there is less chance of it becoming infected. A blister is the body's own way of cooling friction burns to the skin. However, if you are undertaking a lengthy walk it may become necessary to burst the blister. Before you do this, make sure the blister and skin around it is clean. Do this with a sterile wipe (which you should have in your first aid kit).

The next step is to sterilise a clean needle, or small scissors, by heating the tip with a flame, from a match or cigarette lighter. Carefully prick the blister to make a small hole in it. Do not insert the needle deeply – just enough to go through the top covering of the blister. Gently squeeze the fluid out. This should relieve the pressure and it should feel less painful. Don't cut away the skin covering the blister as leaving the top cover of the blister intact helps to prevent infection.

Apply antiseptic cream to the area of the blister and cover with gauze and tape. Avoid simply putting a plaster over as it will not absorb fluid. Pad the area of foot up as much as possible to prevent further friction. Ideally,

you want to keep all pressure off of the blister while it is healing but this is not always possible while out walking.

Like so many things in life, prevention is better than cure. To avoid blisters your boots must fit properly and be comfortable. The wrong boot size is the most common cause of blisters. Make sure the inside lining and innersole are not worn. Wear good quality hillwalking socks that fit properly. Ideally, you should wear two pairs of socks (a thinner sock or liner sock under a pair of thick hillwalking socks) and remember holes in socks cause blisters. If you have bony protrusions, or sensitive skin areas, on your toes or feet, protect them with additional padding.

Recurring blister problems are usually due to abnormal foot structures or gait patterns. Flat feet, feet with very high arches, bunions, and pronation (a rolling out of the feet, so that when you walk you apply excessive force to the inner side of your feet), are all foot problems that can be successfully treated. A visit to the chiropodist will help.

Blisters can be dangerous for people with diabetes, poor circulation or decreased feeling in their feet, those with compromised immune systems, and those with other serious diseases. If you fall into any of these categories, you are advised to see you doctor at the first sign of blister formation.

Finally, on the subject of foot care, make sure you keep your toenails trimmed. Long or jagged nails can dig into neighbouring toes, causing considerable discomfort.

In the event of accident or emergency

Thankfully accidents are rare. But if you should find yourself in the unfortunate position where a member of your family or group is seriously injured or falls ill in the outdoors, the first thing to do is assess the casualty and carry out what first aid you can. Make them as comfortable as possible and ensure they are protected from the elements.

Get to a Rescue Post or telephone, or use a mobile phone (if you are taking a mobile, remember to charge it before you leave). Dial 999 and ask for 'Police'. Give as much information as you can over the telephone so rescuers can find the location of a casualty as quickly as possible. If you are walking in a group send responsible people off the hill – two if possible – to the nearest telephone with the name of the casualty, the location of the casualty (a six figure grid reference), what has happened to them and what first aid treatment has been carried out. It's a good idea to write all this down on a piece of paper at the scene of the accident or emergency and give this to the people sent to raise the alarm. Mark the casualty site as prominently as you can so rescuers can see it, then sit tight.

Check weather forecasts

One important thing to do before you set out is to check the weather forecast. Both the BBC and Grampian and Scottish Television put out forecasts at the end of their news bulletins and you can get up-to-date weather news on local radio, in newspapers and on the internet. Don't be afraid to cancel or curtail a trip if the weather is bad – there's no point going out in vertical rain and having a miserable time, especially when there's always another day. Once out, be prepared to retreat or alter your route if weather conditions deteriorate.

Distress signal

One vital piece of kit to carry is a whistle. If you do get into difficulties on high ground or in remote terrain and find you are unable to move or send for help, you'll need to know the Distress Signal. This consists of six blasts of a whistle, followed by a minute's silence, then another six blasts. This is repeated every minute. If someone (who knows the signal) hears you, he or she will respond with three whistle blasts, followed by a minute's silence, then another three blasts, to confirm. The signal can also be given using a torch. Continue giving the signal at regular intervals so rescuers can locate your position.

These days, it's not uncommon to read about stranded hillwalkers or climbers using a mobile telephone to call for help. By all means pack a mobile phone, but only use it if a real emergency arises and there is no other option. There have been cases of people using mobile phones to summon a mountain rescue team, just because they were tired and hungry.

Another issue to consider is reception. In many of the remoter parts of Scotland you will discover the signal is either not very good, or non-existent, so don't rely on being able to use your mobile, whatever network you are on. If you do take your phone, remember to charge it before you leave home.

Dogs

Dogs love the countryside. But however docile, all have a natural instinct to chase other creatures, whether they are rabbits, sheep or ground nesting birds, like grouse. Man's best friend may be pottering along quite happily beside his owner, but a sudden movement in the bracken or the scent of a grazing animal may be all it takes to trigger this impulse. However obedient, when a dog is in the throes of a chase, the creature's single-minded pursuit means it's very difficult to call him off.

Each year thousands of sheep are killed or injured by dogs and the behaviour of unruly mutts can have an adverse affect on a farmer or landowner's welcome for walkers. Where a walk passes through sheep grazing land, it's always best to keep your dog on the lead. If you don't, bear in mind the law allows farmers and landowners to shoot dogs that are worrying livestock.

Midges

A factor that could affect the enjoyment of your walk, especially in the Highlands and west coast areas of Scotland, is the dreaded midge. This tiny bloodsucking insect can cause havoc with some people, while leaving others virtually untouched. Smearing yourself with crushed bog myrtle is said to help but far better to buy a spray or roll-on repellent if you find yourself on the menu.

KNOW THE COUNTRY CODE

- **Guard against all risk of fire**
- **Keep dogs under proper control**
- **Leave all gates as you find them**
- **Keep to paths across farmland**
- **Avoid damaging fences, hedges and walls**
- **Leave no litter**
- **Safeguard water supplies**
- **Protect wildlife, wild plants and trees**
- **Go carefully on country roads**
- **Respect the life of the countryside**
- **Contact landowners during stalking and other critical periods**

The Scottish countryside is not just a place for recreation. Many people make their living from the land. In Scotland, hillwalkers are free to roam the land with no criminal law of trespass. However, for this to remain the case, consideration has to be given to those who work in the countryside. In this book the walks are all along recognised routes, but you will find there are restrictions on some of the walks, such as requests for dogs to be on the lead if a path or track cuts through land used for sheep grazing, or if a route should be avoided during the stalking season. Most importantly, avoid disturbance to farming and other land management activities when you are out and pay heed to diversion signs that may be in place, for example, in a forest where trees are being felled.

About the walks . . .

The vast majority of walks in this book are circuits so you can start and finish in the same place, normally either in, or close by, a public car park. There are a small number of linear routes that start and finish in different places but these all have regular public transport to return you to the point from where you set off.

All of the walks follow paths and tracks for the majority of the way and these are either rights of way or permissive paths (routes where there is no problem with public access).

Fact files

Every walk in this book has a fact file. This gives the distance of a route in miles and kilometres, a grading and an indication of how much time you should allow for the walk.

It also tells you which map, or maps, you will need to follow the route. Ordnance Survey (OS) 1:50,000 Landranger maps (they've pink covers) are the ones most commonly used by walkers. These are widely available and can be bought in book shops, outdoor shops and tourist information centres. Some of our routes are also covered by Harvey's maps. Produced by a Scottish firm specialising in maps for walkers, these are more detailed than the OS sheets and come in scales of 1:40,000 and 1:25,000. They are waterproof.

The fact file shows you where to start the walk and where to park your car. A six figure grid reference is provided and additional details may be provided here if the journey to the start point is complicated.

Finally, the fact file provides a grading – a brief resume of the terrain, with details of what the route is like on the ground. It will tell you about the type of tracks and paths followed, if there is a fair bit of ascent, and whether sections are steep. There is also information on livestock and the need, where it exists, for dogs to be on the lead. Any restrictions on the route, such as stalking, will be found here.

Timings

It's always difficult to put an exact time on how long a route will take. Everyone walks at a different pace and while some people set off with one eye always on the finishing point, others will spend time stopping to enjoy views, or looking at the flora and fauna. To assist in deciding which walk to choose, we've broken the routes down into three categories, as follows:

Full day walk – This is a route that will take between three and seven hours to complete for a walker going at an average pace.

Half day walk – A route that will take up to three hours to complete and can be completed in a morning, or after lunch.

Short stroll – Short, gentle, low level strolls that will take a couple of hours at most to complete.

Gradings

The routes in this book are divided into three different grades to help you decide which ones are most suited for your level of ability and experience. The gradings are:

Easy – These are short low level walks suitable for families with children over six years of age. They follow good tracks and paths, although comfortable footwear is recommended. It is also a good idea to wear warm clothing and pack waterproofs and some simple refreshments, such as water or juice and snack bars.

Moderate – These are longer walks where a reasonable level of fitness is required, covering both low level and some upland terrain, suitable for adults and children over the age of ten. Hill walking boots and warm clothing should be worn and waterproofs should be packed, along with liquid and some food to keep you going. Walkers should also take the relevant map and a compass and know how to use them.

Challenging – These are the toughies, longer walks for fit adults and accompanied teenage children with a good level of hill walking experience. While there are tracks and paths for the majority of the routes, there may be some sections over rougher, open country. The challenging walks cover upland terrain and mountain peaks, so ascent, some of it quite arduous, is required. These walks call for hill walking boots, warm clothing and waterproofs. You should also have the relevant map and a compass and know how to use them. Take a packed lunch, plus high-energy snacks, such as cereal bars, chocolate, nuts, etc.

Keep the kids happy

To prevent younger children becoming bored on longer walks, introduce some activities to keep them occupied. Perhaps they could gather different leaves, twigs, feathers and other small objects while out and stick these in a scrapbook back home. Encourage them to collect things, like pinecones on a woodland walk, or shells and shiny pebbles on a coastal route. Give them a cheap disposable camera so they can take their own snaps. Pack paper and crayons for bark rubbings, play a game of I-spy as you go, or sing songs. For older children, creating a quiz round map symbols can hold their attention while developing their interest in map reading.

Scottish Hill Tables

For the majority of people who do it, hillwalking is simply a hobby, a way of unwinding at the end of a hectic week. However, like most hobbies, there are those who enjoy having additional incentives and it's here that Scotland's hill tables come into play. These are lists of hills, compiled according to height.

The best known is Munro's Tables, a roll of Scottish mountains over 3000 feet. The original list was drawn up by Sir Hugh Munro and published in 1891. Over the years there have been a number of revisions and the total currently stands at 284.

From this has stemmed the popular pursuit of 'Munro-bagging' – attempting to climb all of the Munros. Some take a lifetime to achieve the goal, while the record for the fastest round – held by Glasgow postman Charlie Campbell – currently stands at an amazing 49 days.

Below the Munros are the Corbetts, a list of Scottish peaks over 2500 feet in height but under 3000 feet with a re-ascent of 500 feet on all sides compiled by Mr J. Rooke Corbett. There are currently 220 but, like the Munros, the table is subject to occasional revision.

Then there are Donald's Tables, listing all hills in the Scottish Lowlands 2000 feet in height and above, originally compiled by Mr Percy Donald. There are currently 89 of these, plus numerous tops.

Finally, for the purposes of this book, there are the Grahams, a complete list of Scottish hills between 2000 and 2499 feet high. The table was compiled by Alan Dawson and Fiona Torbet (née Graham) and contains 224 peaks.

There are a number of Munros, Corbetts, Donalds and Grahams in this book. If you enjoy them and are inspired to do more, the following books will help you get started:

The Munros (Scottish Mountaineering Club)

Munro's Tables and other Tables of Lower Hills (Scottish Mountaineering Club)

The Corbetts and other Scottish Hills (Scottish Mountaineering Club)

The Munro Almanac by Cameron McNeish
The Corbett Almanac by Cameron McNeish
(both published by In Pinn)

IMPORTANT NOTE

All of the routes contained within this book were checked prior to publication. While every care has been taken to ensure the accuracy of the route directions, neither the publisher nor walkscotland.com can accept responsibility for errors or omissions or for changes in details given.

Please bear in mind that developments in the countryside, whether created by man or the elements, can happen without prior warning. Paths can be rerouted, tracks can be temporarily closed (eg: due to forestry felling), fences can be moved and bridges can be washed out.

Every effort will be made to provide details of any changes to any of the routes on the walkscotland.com website. The publisher and **walkscotland.com** accept no responsibility for any accident or injury sustained while following any of the routes published in this book.

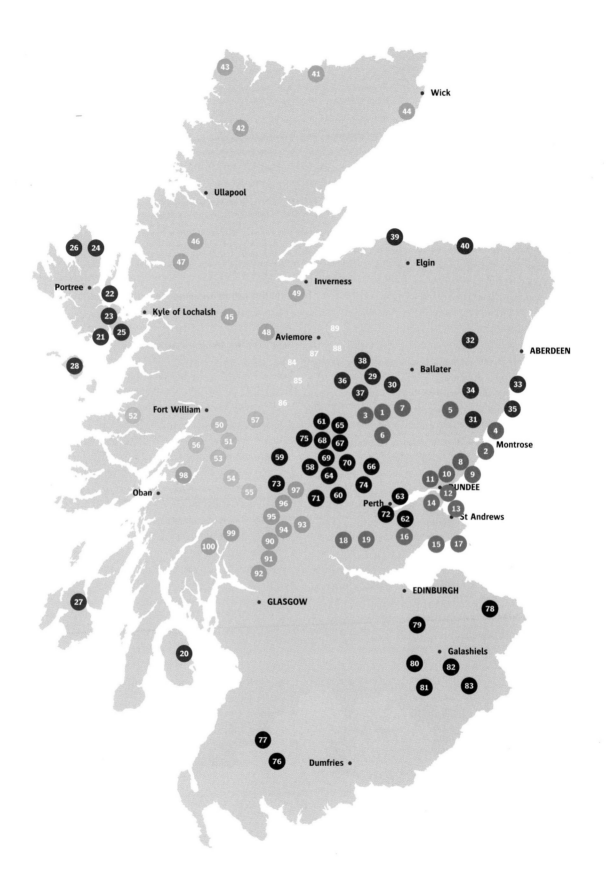

Driesh by Kilbo Path

Most walkers will climb Driesh from Glen Doll, probably linking it with neighbouring Mayar. However, an alternative way to tackle these hills is from the south along an ancient right of way known as the Kilbo Path.

There is parking for a couple of cars a few hundred metres beyond **Glenprosen Lodge** at the foot of a tarmac road leading into **Glenclova Forest**. Don't venture into the forest but follow the road that drops to farm buildings at Runtaleave. Follow the track north west, pass through open fields to arrive at the house at **Old Craig**.

Go through a gate and continue towards Craig Tillelet. The burn, which has been gurgling away on your left, is crossed via a substantial bridge before you pass through a forestry gate. On the current OS map it indicates that the path here is bounded on both sides by trees but in fact the area to your right has been felled.

The path continues to skirt the plantation and soon the crumbled stone ruin of **Kilbo** appears ahead. It makes an excellent picnic spot and is reached by continuing along the path and through another gate where you can cross the water safely by a metal girder. A signpost here points you in the direction of Glen Clova and the track disappears into the trees.

The first real climbing of the day is done here as you make you way up through the woods towards Cairn Dye. The path leaves the woods and emerges into open heath where another signpost points in the direction of Glen Clova. Continue up the **Shank of Drumwhallo** to reach the long ridge between **Mayar** and **Driesh** where yet another signpost appears. Turn right and follow the line of the fence towards the western face of Driesh. You have to lose some height before you can begin climbing the rocky path that, especially in wet or misty weather, requires a bit of care.

You will pass a stone cairn before the substantial stone circle surrounding the peak's trig point comes into view.

From the summit, the easiest route back to Glenprosen Lodge is to retrace your steps. An alternative way to continue the walk is to head in an easterly direction and climb to the top of the Hill of Strone.

A wooden post surrounded by a small cairn marks the summit and the end of the day's climbing. It's downhill from here on in as you head off towards Glenclova Forest. Head southwest from the summit, past a line of shooting butts, and into the woods via a large gap in the boundary fence.

After a while the path emerges from the trees and into a clearing where you should continue left, keeping the small burn on your right hand side. The track enters the woods again and eventually ends at the gate near where you should have parked your car.

12 miles/19km

Challenging, full day walk

A long track walk, followed by a fairly strenuous ascent. Suitable for experienced adult hillwalkers and teenage children. The ascent and descent of Driesh is quite steep so proper footwear is a must. In winter it is a more serious proposition and when the mountain is under snow, this is a route for experienced hillwalkers with crampons and ice-axes and the knowledge to use them.

Map: OS Landranger, sheet 44.

Start/Parking: Entrance gate at Glenclova Forest, Glen Prosen. GR: NO 290681.

Log on to this walk at:
www.walkscotland.com/route1

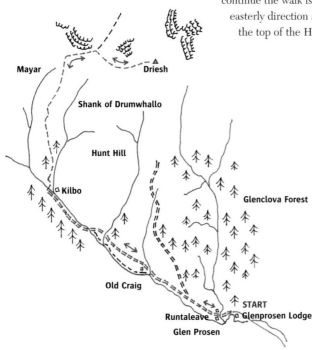

Lunan Bay to Ethie Haven

For a perfect summer stroll head for Lunan Bay on the Angus coast. The two mile-long swath of golden sand stretches between steep, craggy headlands where the North Sea breakers roll in. Perched above the dunes is the dramatic sandstone ruin of Red Castle and, further along, a pair of tiny hamlets forgotten by the passage of time.

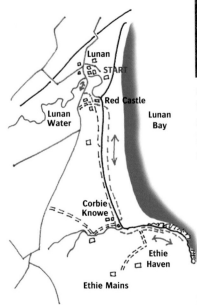

Head out of the **Lunan Bay** car park, back up the access track to the hamlet of **Lunan**. When you reach the road, turn left and follow it south, past the entrance to Lunan House Nursing Home and then a church and graveyard. The road bends sharp left to cross the **Lunan Water** by an old stone bridge. Stay with the tree-lined lane as it skirts between open fields to a copse of tall trees where a path bears left.

This rises quite steeply, passing through a metal gate, to **Red Castle**. The elevated position affords fine views north over the twisting mouth of the Lunan Water, and east out to sea.

The path skirts between the two main portions of the castle before descending steeply to the sandy beach below. Stay to the left of the cottages. Once on the sand, walk along the south bank of the Lunan Water towards the sea, then bear right and follow the beach south.

A wide expanse of white sand stretches into the distance towards the headland at **Ethie Haven**. The walking is easiest if you stick to the hard sand near the waters' edge. You have to cross a couple of small streams and, as the field on the right below the farm at Redcastle gives way to a rougher slope of grass and gorse, you can see the squat lines of a bomb-proof brick and concrete war-time look out post embedded into the slope.

About half a mile from here is **Corbie Knowe**, a rustic settlement of beach huts, cabins and caravans. Head up the beach to a small parking area and, between two large concrete blocks on the left, a narrow gravel path leads to a wooden footbridge over a burn. Cross, and a path rises behind the huts to the top of the cliffs, skirting above the south end of the bay to join a farm track.

The track soon descends to Ethie Haven, a hamlet of stone cottages built to house fishermen and their families. Time has passed this place by, to the extent that mains electricity only reached Ethie Haven within the last few years.

You can make your way a little further along the coast by following a grassy path below a line of wooden huts to a couple of tiny pebble beaches sheltered under the headland beyond. Here the route ends and the best way back is to retrace your steps. At low water it is possible to paddle over the mouth of the Lunan Water, thereby cutting out the climb up to Red Castle and the trek along the road back to the car park.

 6 miles/10km

Easy, half day walk

Low level coastal walk along sandy beach and path. Suitable for all ages and abilities. Take care on the cliff-top path above Corbie Knowe as there is a fairly long drop. When there are extremely high tides, it may be necessary to swap the beach for a track running along the edge of the field above the sand.

Map: OS Landranger, sheet 54.

Start/Parking: Lunan Bay public car park, Lunan.
GR: NO 692515

Log on to this walk at:
www.walkscotland.com/route2

Ben Gulabin

Glen Shee is ski country. However, when the snow has left the slopes it's the walkers who have all the fun. At the head of the glen is Ben Gulabin (806 metres), a prominent peak rising above the tiny hamlet of Spittal of Glenshee. The ascent is short but strenuous and an excellent way to get to know the area better.

The starting point for this walk is less than a mile north of the **Spittal**, which sits at the head of the glen, on the junction of the burns flowing down Gleann Beag and Glen Lochsie to form the **Shee Water**.

Leave the parking area on the A93 at a gate and, once through, follow the track as it heads north, rising diagonally across the eastern slope of the hill and below the crags of Carn Dubh. It curves round the hillside to cross a burn before rising more steeply.

As you approach the col above, the track nears the remains of a ruined hut and some old metalwork associated with an early ski development. These days the glen's winter sports activities are located further up the valley at the Glenshee Ski

Area, one of Scotland's five main ski centres.

At this point, cross the burn and follow a tributary upstream, a grassy path cutting its way through the heather to emerge on to a wide ridge. Bear right here and climb the final short distance to the summit.

Ben Gulabin is a Corbett, a Scottish peak over 2500 feet in height but under 3000 feet with a re-ascent of 500 feet on all sides. The name is Gaelic and translates as either hill of the curlew, or hill of the peak.

The top offers views north to

The Cairnwell – an easy Munro to identify due to the tall aerial mast on the summit – and across the glen to Glas Maol and Creag Leacach. To the south-east **Glen Shee** stretches off into the distance towards Blairgowrie and the fertile lands of Strathmore.

Over to the west is Glas Tulaichean and, below it, Glen Lochsie. Surprising as it may seem, this remote glen was once home to a railway line! The tracks were laid not long after Sir Archibald Birkmyre, who made his money with the Greenock Rope Company, moved into Dalmunzie House in the early part of the 20th century.

As he was enlarging the property, he built the line in 1921 to bring stone down from a quarry up the glen and it was later used to ferry guests up to a smaller lodge at the top of Glen Lochsie, where a tiny station platform was created and still existing, hidden in the heather. The rails have since been lifted, but the trackbed up Glen Lochsie can still be traced and is an enjoyable walk in its own right.

To finish this walk, retrace your steps from the summit of Ben Gulabin back to the start.

2.5 miles/4km
Moderate, half day walk
A short but strenuous climb. The walk passes through grazing land, so dogs should be on the lead.

Map: OS Landranger, sheet 43.

Start/Parking: Roadside gate on the A93 a mile north of Spittal of Glenshee. There is space for a number of cars but please don't block the gate.
GR: NO 114715.

Log on to this walk at:
www.walkscotland.com/route3

Montrose Bay

The Angus coast is a wonderful place to wander. There's so much to savour – from long strips of golden sand lurking between steep craggy headlands where seabirds roost, to quiet, calm rivers meandering through leafy woodlands. The county is one of the sunniest parts of Scotland – Met Office records support this claim – and Montrose Bay is an ideal introduction to the delights that await the walker.

Esk and the **River North Esk**. Leave the car park at **South Links** and head across the road, out on to the beach. Walk north along the beach until you reach the mouth of the River North Esk where huge flocks of seabirds are often to be seen resting on sandbanks.

As you approach this point, the dunes on the left start to get smaller. Leave the beach and climb over them, then descend towards the riverbank. A short way inland, you'll join a track which runs west, crossing a small wooden bridge. Continue to reach the corner of woodland where you'll pass through a gate. The way runs alongside the river, passing a compound of rusty old tanks and a cottage to reach a small fisherman's bothy. Turn left on the road past Fisherhills and, at the next junction, go left on a track leading east back towards the sea. It skirts between two coniferous plantations to reach a junction just short of a salmon station.

Turn right here and follow the track to the edge of woodland on the left. It is possible to continue straight on along the track here but it is more pleasant if you bear left and follow the fence along the edge of the trees towards the dunes. At the bottom corner of the trees, turn right and walk south between the plantation and the dunes. At the end of a long clearing, you'll pass by some buildings. Continue straight on along the edge of

7.5 miles/12km
Moderate, half day walk
Flat route along sandy beach, track and path. Suitable for adults and older children.

Map: OS Landranger, sheet 45, 54.

Start/Parking: South Links, Montrose. GR: NO 727580.
Plenty of free parking.

Log on to this walk at:
www.walkscotland.com/route4

the woodland and, at the end, turn right, a sandy path leading down to a stile in the corner of the fence.

Cross the stile and walk over a piece of rough ground to reach a substantial concrete track. This formed one of the taxiways of the wartime **airfield** located here. At a gate on the left, head into the golf course – a path skirts along the edge of the links, passing by a driving range on the right. Rejoin the surfaced road at another of the gates and follow it out to join the public road just beyond a civic amenity site.

Turn left into Broomfield Road. Beyond a set of bollards at the far end, head left on a surfaced path occupying the trackbed of an old railway. This runs by a paddling pool and play park to reach the golf course clubhouse. Join the public road in front of this, turn left and follow the road back to the car park.

River North Esk

Kinnaber Links

Former airfield

Montrose

Golf course

South Links

Montrose Bay

River South Esk

A92

The first stretch of the route is along the town's main beach, stretching between the estuary of the **River South**

Mount Battock

Mount Battock, above Glen Esk, is the country's most easterly Corbett and for fairly fit hillwalkers it's a relatively easy climb at any time of the year. For families, however, a good clear spring or summer day is perhaps the best time to launch an assault on the summit.

Set off up the track as it rises gently to an old stone mill building with green painted doors and windows. The way curves left, skirting the edge of woodland, to reach a cottage and outbuildings at **Mill of Aucheen**. A short way on, you'll meet a junction. Turn right and the track skirts along in front of a small cottage to reach a gate. Go through and follow the track as it stays close to the edge of the field, heading towards more woodland.

Ignore a gated track on the right and follow the route along the northern edge of the plantation. At the bottom of the steep tree-covered bank on the right the wide and shallow sweep of the Burn of Turret flows down, destined for the **River North Esk**.

The track dips beyond the end of the woodland to reach a gate. Beyond this it reaches a stream. There's a pair of footbridges to the right.

On the other side, the track rises once more and crosses an open field. Carry on through another gate at the end of the field to reach a junction of tracks. Go left here and climb over open heather moorland. Pass through a gate higher up and, in a short distance, the track curves right and climbs round the southern flank of **Allrey**.

The way heads north to reach **Black Burn**. There is no bridge at the crossing point but it is quite shallow and is easy to get across. A short walk up the track there's a small wooden shelter.

From the hut the climb becomes harder as you rise on to Mount Battock's outlying top. The track serves a series of grouse butts scattered over the higher ground and you will soon reach a fence running west to east. This is well placed as a navigational aid as it runs over the 717 metre spot height and then down into the col. It rises over the western flank of **Mount Battock**, guiding you right on to the top, where a trig point and cairn are to be found.

Navigating your way down is easy thanks to the presence of a fence. Follow the posts and wire south from the top, descending into a wide col, then there's an easy climb on to **Hill of Saughs**. The boundary fence leads into the pass

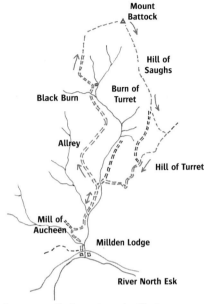

between Hill of Saughs and Hill of Fingray, meeting up with a track. Turn right and follow this down over **Hill of Turret**. It makes a sharp right turn and descends through a gate to a wooden footbridge over the **Burn of Turret**. The way rises up the bank on the other side to reach the junction of tracks where you branched off earlier in the day. Retrace your steps from here to the start.

9 miles/14.4km
Challenging, full day walk

A straightforward route for fairly fit hillwalkers and older children with a strenuous ascent. Dogs need to be on the lead in places due to sheep and/or cattle grazing.

Map: OS Landranger, sheet 44.

Start/Parking: BT phonebox adjacent to the Glen Esk road by Millden Lodge. GR: NO 540789. There is space for a few cars, so arrive early.

**Log on to the
www.**

Mount Blair

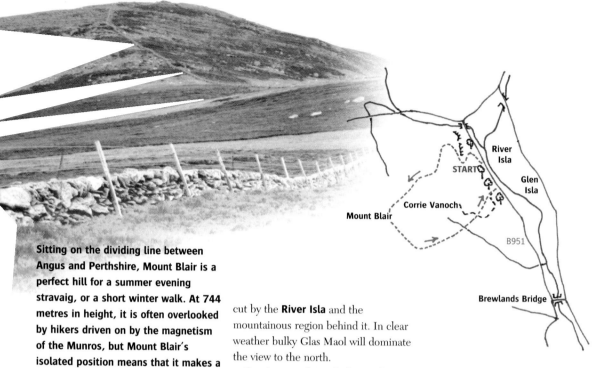

Sitting on the dividing line between Angus and Perthshire, Mount Blair is a perfect hill for a summer evening stravaig, or a short winter walk. At 744 metres in height, it is often overlooked by hikers driven on by the magnetism of the Munros, but Mount Blair's isolated position means that it makes a perfect viewing platform for the bigger hills of Glen Shee to the north.

Parking is available at the small car park near **Altaltan**. Go through a metal gate at the back of the parking area, leading into a copse of woodland and follow a path up through the trees. Keep your eyes peeled as you may be lucky enough to spot deer foraging among the fallen leaves.

The path takes a meandering route towards the upper reaches of **Cor̲̲̲̲noch**. The adventurous can opt̲̲̲̲ ̲̲̲̲scent by picking a line ̲̲̲̲s. Climbing hills in ̲̲̲̲tages and ̲̲̲̲remely ̲̲̲̲ticularly ̲̲̲̲best

cut by the **River Isla** and the mountainous region behind it. In clear weather bulky Glas Maol will dominate the view to the north.

Continue on the path that curls its way up towards the secondary summit and a large cairn which sits at 653 metres. The track strikes towards the main summit and it is comforting to know that a line of old fence posts is there to show the way should the clouds suddenly descend.

The tramp towards the top crosses

4 miles/6.4km
Moderate, half day walk

The choice of a scramble if you opt for a direct ascent of Corrie Vanoch, or a leisurely stroll if you follow the path. A fine walk suitable for all ages and abilities.

Map: OS Landranger, sheet 43.

̲̲̲art/Parking: Small car park just off ̲̲̲B951. GR: NO 185633

this walk at:
̲̲̲tland.com/route6

patches of standing water, likely to be hard frost in winter, so be careful and skirt round their edges where the going will be less treacherous.

The path steepens as you near the summit and once or twice you may want to use your hands as you approach the upper reaches.

The summit of Mount Blair is occupied by a telecommunications tower and associated paraphernalia and, although it does take away from the beauty of the hill, it doesn't spoil the panorama unfolding all around.

A semi-circular stone shelter erected just a short distance away from the summit trig point provides a handy spot to take some lunch and listen to the eerie whining of the wind as it reverberates through the metal pylons. Descent is a simple matter of retracing your steps but the walk can be extended by taking routes down along the county boundary between Angus and Perth and Kinross in either direction.

Loch Brandy

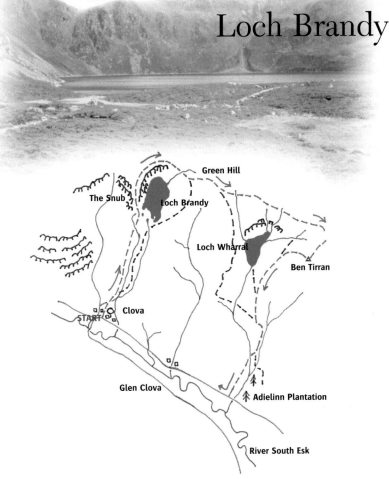

Seek out the scenic delights of a hidden lochan on this circular route that starts and finishes in the tiny village of Clova. The walk offers some stunning panoramas over one of the finest glens in Angus and, while there is some hard work involved, the effort is well rewarded.

Leave the car park, turn right and follow the minor road west over a narrow stone bridge spanning the Corrie Burn to reach the Clova Hotel. The way passes through a gravel car park to the right of the building. At a sign for 'Public footpath to Glenesk' it continues through a small copse of woodland, emerging on to open hillside beyond.

The path crosses a stile and here begins the steady climb north over moor. As you rise, great views open up below of the fertile plains of **Glen Clova**, the **River South Esk** looping its way through green fields with sheep and cattle. Prepare yourself for another short pull higher up. The effort is worth it when you rise over the lip of the coire and see **Loch Brandy** for the first time. Before you, a deep pool of dark water snuggles in the curving arms of rock that rise up steeply from the quiet shores. Loch Brandy is said to be the only site in Scotland where a very rare, tiny bright orange water creature called the diatom is found.

Take a well deserved rest by the water, then continue up the path through heather on to **The Snub**, a craggy shoulder separating Loch Brandy to the right and Corrie of Clova to the left. There are steep drops on both sides so take care. Admiring the scenery is always a good excuse if you need to pause for breath here.

At the top of The Snub the path flattens out to reveal a wide, open plain ahead. The remote landscape is frequented by herds of red deer and wild mountain hare. You might also spot grouse, ptarmigan and, in spring and summer, the elusive dotterel. The path skirts right, following the top of the coire round with steep cliffs below.

As you continue above Loch Brandy, the path reaches a junction. Go left to the summit of **Green Hill**, an unremarkable little hump in the heather, then continue over open moor to reach the top of **Ben Tirran**. Head south over the shoulder and pick out the path down to **Loch Wharrel**, a popular spot with pike fishermen. From the southern-most point of the lochan, an obvious path descends to the **Adielinn Plantation** and a path skirts down the side of the trees. Continue down to the road, or turn right just before you reach the road on another path that rises and falls over a series of low mounds. This runs parallel with the road for a way, then reaches a pond hidden in the trees. On the far side, it curves round to join the B955. Follow this back to Clova.

9 miles/14.5km
Challenging, full day walk
Good paths with a strenuous climb. Suitable for fairly fit hillwalkers and older children. Take care on the sections above Loch Brandy and Loch Wharrel and do not go too close to the edge as there are long, steep drops.

Map: OS Landranger, sheet 44.

Start/Parking: Public car park, with toilets and picnic area, opposite the Clova Hotel. GR: NO 327731.

Log on to this walk at:
www.walkscotland.com/route7

St Vigeans Nature Trail

One of the most picturesque churches in Scotland is the starting point for a quiet saunter along an old railway line. The St Vigeans Nature Trail sets off from the tiny village of St Vigeans, dominated by an impressive sandstone church sitting atop a small hill in the centre of the community. Below, in the crescent of quaint little cottages, is a museum, housing a collection of Pictish artifacts.

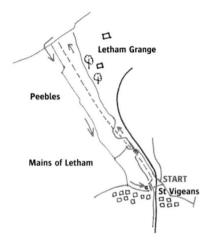

The trail, lined with trees and shrubs that are home to birds and foxes, runs through predominantly open country. Accompanied for much of the way by a bubbling wee stream, it skirts by **Letham Grange**, a hotel boasting its own golf course.

From the car park, cross a stone bridge over the burn and head towards the church. Turn right beyond an area of grass with a park bench and enter a small cemetery. The way runs through a grove of neatly clipped yew trees to reach a wooden footbridge over the burn on the right. Cross and immediately turn left, joining the line of the old railway. It heads north, running parallel with the burn. The peaceful path skirts through shrubs to emerge on to a road at a fine stone bridge over the burn. An old mill here has been renovated into a house.

Cross the road and rejoin the trackbed. It continues north, passing by the entrance to a house. Beyond this, the way skirts behind a row of new houses before passing through a cutting and under an old railway bridge. At the end of the cutting, views open out over a golf course on the right, to Letham Grange.

The path arrives at the remains of an old station and, a few yards on, joins a road. If you want to avoid road walking, retrace your steps along the nature trail. However, to create a circuit, turn left and follow the road up through a deep cutting. Ignore the entrance to East Mains of Colliston Farm, on the right, and turn left at the next road junction. A quiet country road, lined with leafy deciduous woodland, heads south,

dipping before curving up between open fields. Carry straight on at the next junction, staying with the road, to reach **Peebles Farm**.

On from here are the remains of an old wartime airfield in the form of hangers now used to store farm machinery and straw. This was connected to the Royal Marines Condor base, which was a naval aerodrome during WWII. Continue south, ignoring a track on the left, and the way continues to be flanked by open crop fields. The route skirts the high rear perimeter fence of RM Condor to reach a junction at **Mains of Letham**. Don't turn left but carry straight on past a pair of cottages and through a farm.

The road curves left and then right, running straight alongside strawberry fields. When you reach St Vigeans Manse (a modern bungalow), turn left, and a short section of roadway leads to the minor road back down to **St Vigeans**.

5 miles/8km
Easy, half day walk
A low level walk along an old railway trackbed and quiet country roads. Suitable for all ages and abilities. Take care and keep an eye out for traffic on the road section of the walk.

Map: OS Landranger, sheet 54.

Start/Parking: St Vigeans Church, Arbroath. GR: NO 640429. There's a public car park on the opposite side of the burn. This is reached by following Brechin Road out of Arbroath. Beyond houses on the left, turn left on the road signed for St Vigeans then left again where the road dips. A narrow lane runs under the railway line to reach the car park, on the left.

Log on to this walk at:
www.walkscotland.com/route8

Arbroath Cliffs

Seaton Den

Carlingheugh Bay

East Seaton

Arbroath

The Deil's Heid

Dickmont's Den

START

The cliff trail north of Arbroath is awash with fascinating rock formations, christened with evocative names such as the Deil's Heid, Seaman's Grave and Mermaid's Kirk. It's a bracing coastal walk skirting the swirling sea that can be enjoyed at any time of the year. In the culinary world, Arbroath is best known for its smokies, a smoked haddock dish that originated in the nearby village of Auchmithie. These are available from local fish merchants and can be eaten cold straight from the wrapper.

The walk starts at the east end of Victoria Park, next to public toilets at Whiting Ness. A surfaced path climbs on to the top of the red sandstone cliffs. It levels out quickly and skirts between open fields on the left and the sea to the right. The path is not far from the edge, so take care.

About half a mile from the start is the Needle E'e, a rock with a narrow hole cut through it. A short way on the path curves left to loop round above **Dickmont's Den**, a deep, narrow inlet where the sea bubbles and froths below. Continue round the channel and the path is reunited with the cliff top. Further on you can't miss the **Deil's Heid**, an impressive sea stack. The path

curves left round the headland here to reach **Carlingheugh Bay**, a wide sweep of sandy and pebbled beach.

On the right a small path drops down to the beach. The route continues straight on here, but the short detour is well worth making. There is a sea arch at the south end of the shoreline and a couple of caves to explore at the north end, one going right through the headland. The bay is also a fine spot for a picnic.

Back on the cliff top path, the way heads inland, leaving the sea behind, and continues into the woods of **Seaton Den**. Within the trees, the route drops to cross a small stream, then rises gently through the peaceful glade, a mix of deciduous trees, broom and gorse.

At the top you emerge on to a quiet country road. Turn left and follow this road to its next junction. Go left again and stay with the road as it skirts a strip of woodland to reach a track on the left, signed for Seaton Estates. Follow this down past Seaton Estate Caravan Park. The entrance is on the right – don't go in but carry on until you reach **East Seaton** farm at the bottom.

At the farm, turn right and then left a few yards on, beyond a big house. A track leads towards the sea, following the farmhouse garden wall past a small cottage. Carry straight on through a metal barrier gate and the track passes between open fields, curving left. At the next junction, turn right to rejoin the coastal path at Dickmont's Den. Go right here and retrace your steps along the cliff-top trail to reach Victoria Park.

4 miles/6.5km
Easy, half day walk
A level walk which can be enjoyed by all ages at all times of the year but take great care along the cliffs, particularly with young children and dogs, as there is a long, steep drop.

Map: OS Landranger, sheet 54.

Start/Parking: Whiting Ness, Victoria Park. GR: NO 658412.

Log on to this walk at:
www.walkscotland.com/route9

Crombie Reservoir

Crombie Reservoir owes its existence to the once grimy Victorian industrial heart of Dundee – some 10 miles away. But it's hard to believe such a tranquil spot could have ever been so closely linked with the city famously built on jute, jam and journalism. The man-made loch no longer provides Dundee with water, as it did for over a century, and the area is now a country park.

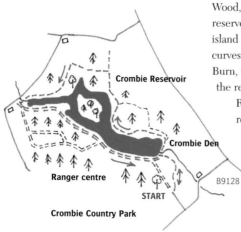

From the car park, follow a path to the right of a wooden cabin, signed for Birch Wood Woodland Walk. Wander through an area of young saplings, the steep slope on the right plunging into **Crombie Den**. The path climbs gently to the dam at the head of the reservoir.

Turn right and cross a bridge over the concrete overflow. Head across the dam to the far end where there's a small wooden hut used by anglers. Go left and follow a good gravel footpath between the skinny trunks of tall Scots Pine trees. This part of the route follows the waymarked Discovery Trail and there are various information panels along the path.

The woodland is home to a wide variety of flora and fauna. Among the creatures you may be lucky enough to spot are red squirrels, roe deer, foxes and green woodpeckers while wild flowers and fungi occupy the forest floor. Out on the water moorhen, grebes and coots lurk in the reeds. Originally dominated by conifers, more recent planting around the shores of the man-made loch has seen evergreens replaced by native species such as oak, alder, rowan and hazel.

The way passes through Crombie East Wood, skirting the northern shore of the reservoir, then bears right as the wooded island offshore is reached. The path soon curves left, crossing the Hyndcastle Burn, to arrive at the reedy west tip of the reservoir.

Remain on the path as it curves round to the southern side of the water. The reservoir was created in the 1860s to provide water for Dundee. Building the dam flooded an old quarry and part of Crombie Den. The reservoir latterly served Carnoustie before it was decommissioned in the 1980s and made into a country park.

During the autumn and winter of 2001/2002, the reservoir's owner, Angus Council, took the unusual step of draining it completely to carry out a major programme of maintenance and repair.

The path soon joins a track heading east through Fallaws Wood to reach the **ranger centre** where you'll find various nature displays and information boards.

The quickest way back to the car park is by the surfaced road. However, the Tree Trail on the right makes an enjoyable detour. Waymarked from the ranger centre, it includes a selection of specimen trees planted as part of the original reservoir landscaping. These include Yew, Douglas Fir, Chile Pine and Eastern Red Cedar.

3 miles/5km
Easy, half day walk
A low-level woodland walk for all ages and abilities. No dogs are allowed in the park, except guide dogs. The park is open from 9am to dusk (9pm in the summer), throughout the year.

Map: OS Landranger, sheet 54.

Start/Parking: Crombie Country Park car park. There is a parking charge. GR: NO 529402.

Log on to this walk at:
www.walkscotland.com/route10

Sidlaw Hills

The Sidlaw Hills may just be a stone's throw from the urban sprawl of Dundee, but in terms of their environment, they are a world away. For centuries these low hills have offered city dwellers a much sought after escape from the hustle and bustle of everyday life.

A public car park opposite **Old Balkello** is a convenient starting point for this walk. On the northern edge of this, a gate leads to an information board with details of a short nature trail laid out amid the young trees. The walk follows this in part.

Bear left and follow a grassy track that skirts along the top edge of an area of open grass. This rises gently to pass through a gap in a neat stone wall. A few yards on, the way reaches a junction. Turn right here and the path rises more steeply, passing under a line of overhead electricity pylons to reach the top edge of the plantation.

Turn right here to join a more established track, then turn left and follow this up to a picnic table below old quarry workings. A path rises from here to reach a gate. To make the short detour to the summit of **Auchterhouse Hill**, go through the gate and turn left.

A wide path rises through bracken and heather to the top, the site of an ancient hill fort. Retrace your steps back to the gate, go through and follow a path that heads north, following the fence up to the col between Auchterhouse Hill and Balkello Hill. At the highest point of the pass, a path branches off on the right, climbing steeply before flattening off to reach a cairn and indicator on the top.

The next port of call – neighbouring **Craigowl Hill** – is clearly seen to the east. This peak is easily identifiable by the jumble of masts adorning its summit.

A narrow path strikes north through the heather from the cairn, meeting up with the boundary fence. It curves right and dips steeply into a narrow glen below. At the bottom, a stile is crossed before the path rises, a strenuous climb leading up past a lone tree to another stile just below the compound of communications equipment.

Cross this and, a short distance on you will reach a cairn. There's a trig-point sandwiched between two fenced enclosures a few metres away.

To begin the descent, recross the stile just below the summit and a path bears left, dropping across the southern slope of Craigowl Hill. It descends through hill grazing country to reach a stile at the bottom. Cross to join a substantial track and turn left, following this as it curves right through a tight bend.

At the next hairpin below, leave the track on the right and follow a grassy path leading down and back into the community woodland. At the bottom, turn left and the route rises gently over a wide grassy gap in the trees, bearing right through saplings to the car park.

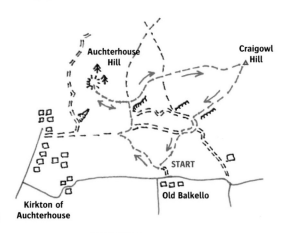

5 miles/8km
Moderate, half day walk
A short walk with some fairly strenuous sections of ascent. Sheep and cattle grazing, so dogs will need to go on the lead in places.

Map: OS Landranger, sheet 54.

Start/Parking: Balkello Community Woodland car, a mile and a half east of Kirkton of Auchterhouse. GR: NO 365385.

Log on to this walk at:
www.walkscotland.com/route11

Tentsmuir Forest

Tentsmuir Forest's network of tracks was created to allow the movement of wood. However, it is also great for walkers, mountain-bikers and pony trekking enthusiasts. Starting on the shores of the wide Tay estuary and continuing through the trees, this route concentrates on the northern section of the plantation and can be undertaken on foot or two wheels.

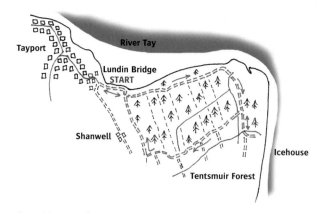

5.3 miles/8.5km

Easy, half day walk

Level forest circuit with tracks throughout. This route is suitable for all ages and abilities and can be undertaken on mountain bikes.

Map: OS Landranger, sheet 59.

Start/Parking: Lundin Bridge, Tayport. GR: NO 466279.

Log on to this walk at:
www.walkscotland.com/route12

Begin at **Lundin Bridge**, on the eastern edge of Tayport. A grassy car park is provided here, opposite a small factory. Cross Lundin Bridge and follow a wide track running along above the shore of the **River Tay**, offering views across the water to Dundee and the coast of Angus. About 300 metres on, the way reaches a fork. Take the left and continue below the fenced compound of a former meteorological station. Beyond this, the track curves right to enter **Tentsmuir Forest**, below a war-time bunker.

Beyond a gate and just inside the plantation, the way reaches another junction. Turn left here and follow the forest road through tall pine trees. It passes a couple of tracks on the right – ignore these – before entering a wide clearing. Carry on along the track and it soon disappears back into the trees. Further tracks appear from time to time but ignore these and stay on the main route. As the track begins to curve right through a wide sweep, it touches the edge of the plantation where a short detour can be made for another view across the Tay.

Back on the track, follow it south, crossing a burn a short distance on. It emerges from the trees at another wide clearing and becomes rather sandy underfoot, indicating that there's a beach not far away.

Walk south until you reach the next junction. Another short detour can be made here. Go straight on to reach a 19th century **icehouse** on the left. This was used to store salmon netted in the sea and, on the opposite side of the forest road, almost obscured by trees and shrubbery, there's a small pond from which ice was taken. To the south of the icehouse, there's a track heading east towards the coast. It crosses a stile next to a wooden gate and emerges at the dunes above Tentsmuir Sands just beyond a small concrete building.

Retrace your steps from here to the junction to the north of the icehouse and turn left. The track goes west into the heart of the forest. Ignore tracks on the left and right and carry straight on. When the track reaches the western boundary of the forest, turn right. A wide grassy track leads north, bounded by an open field on the left. This way is not quite as solid as the more substantial forest roads and can be muddy.

However, it's a peaceful stretch through a mix of trees and shrubbery, lined with broom bushes. At the far end, the track curves right to reach the junction at the edge of the forest. Leave the plantation and follow the track back to Lundin Bridge.

Kinshaldy Beach

Rolling North Sea breakers crashing on to Tentsmuir Sands give way to the peace and tranquillity of a woodland full of wildlife. Situated between the estuaries of the Tay and Eden rivers, Tentsmuir Forest covers 1500 hectares and was acquired by the Forestry Commission in the 1920s. Planted predominantly with Scots and Corsican Pine, it is home to roe deer, red squirrels, butterflies and birds. Bats are also to be found here and special boxes have been put up on the tall trees to encourage growing populations of natterers, pipistrelle and brown long-eared bats.

Set out from the public car park at **Kinshaldy**, three miles drive from Leuchars. A wide path takes you out on to **Tentsmuir Sands**. Turn left and walk north along the beach. A mile on look out for an old wartime look-out post on the dunes. Close by there is a small concrete bunker set into the ground. Take a detour to the tower and enjoy the view from the top. There's a second outpost a little further on. Out to sea you may spot grey seals and oystercatchers on the sandbanks.

As you near **Tentsmuir Point**, a mile beyond the second tower, climb on to the dunes, keeping a post and wire fence on your left. Stay with this to a point where it turns at right angles and runs west. Over by the tree line there are concrete blocks, a wartime effort to stop any invading tanks coming up the beach. On this walk you may also hear, and see, a more modern military presence – jets taking off from RAF Leuchars. Rather than follow the beach round the point, where channels and pools of water are obstacles, it is worth cutting the corner and following the fence overland. Stay with the fence until you pick up the beach again, then head up to the north-east corner of **Tentsmuir Forest**. Just inside the trees there's a track. Follow this west as it marches deep into the trees. In a few hundred yards a track branches off to the left – don't take this. Instead carry on until you reach the next track on the left – follow this south.

There's a green post with the number '34' on it at the junction. The way stretches out in front, running through patches of tall, slender pine, recently felled forest and young conifer saplings. In a mile the track reaches a crossroad.

Go straight on, crossing the Powrie Burn. Although Tentsmuir Forest is dominated by evergreens, there are also silver birch and beech and, at ground level, a colourful patchwork of bracken, broom, lichens and heather.

The track eventually emerges on to the surfaced access road to Kinshaldy car park. Turn left and, in a few metres, you are back where you started.

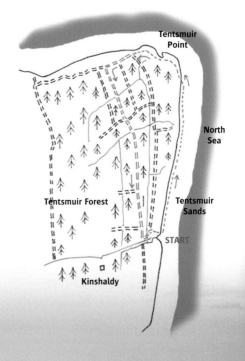

7 miles/11km
Easy, half day walk
Level walking along sandy beach and good forest tracks. Swimming in the sea is not advised due to strong undercurrents and don't venture too far out on to sand bars as they can quickly become cut off by the incoming tide.

Map: OS Landranger, sheet 59.

Start/Parking: Kinshaldy beach car park. GR: NO 498243. There is a parking charge.

Log on to this walk at:
www.walkscotland.com/route13

Wormit to Balmerino

The tiny village of Balmerino in north Fife grew up around a 13th century abbey, located on the gently sloping fertile agricultural banks of the River Tay. The Cistercian monastery was established by William the Lion's widow, Ermengarde, in the early part of the 13th century.

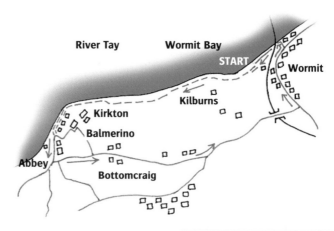

From **Wormit Bay**, walk west on a track along the shore above a narrow shingle beach on the right and a gently rolling field on the left. At the end, a sign for **Balmerino** points the way up a narrow path, rising through bushes to a metal kissing gate. Go through and continue.

The path skirts by sharp strands of gorse and can be muddy here. It soon emerges into an open field. Go through another kissing gate a short way on. Views open out over the Firth of Tay to Dundee on the far bank. Stay close to the fence on the right and beyond another kissing gate, the path drops into a dip, crossing a rather muddy burn.

Below the farm steading at **Kilburns** the path sticks to the fence as it skirts along the edge of a field and at the end of this land has been given over to tree-planting. Pass through a wooden gate with a sign pointing back to Wormit. Continue into another long grassy field that is also planted with saplings.

6 miles/10km

Easy, half day walk
Low-level paths over open fields, muddy in places, and quiet country roads.

Map: OS Landranger, sheet 54 or 59.

Start/Parking: Wormit Bay, at the bottom of Bay Road, Wormit. GR: NO 392259.

Log on to this walk at:
www.walkscotland.com/route14

Go through a gate at the far end and follow a narrow path between a fenced field and a sharp drop to the beach on the right. The path emerges into the open at another gate. Continue from here above the rock foreshore, walking along the front of a cluster of neatly painted waterfront houses.

The track curves left to meet the public road that climbs through Balmerino to the ruins of **Balmerino Abbey**. After visiting the abbey, follow the road south, past a courtyard of cottages. At the top, turn left by the bus shelter and follow the road east, passing through the little hamlet of **Bottomcraig**. The road continues through a leafy avenue, passing the gates of Naughton House and, beyond cottages at Little Inch, it reaches a junction.

Turn left and the road continues east between open fields. Ignore the track on the left leading to Peacehill Farm and remain with the road as it rises over the railway line and meets the B946.

Turn left, heading north, and follow the pavement along the front of a long row of houses. Wormit Farm is on the left and then the road curves right into **Wormit** proper. Continue until you

reach a play park on the left, to the east end of the Tay Railway Bridge.

Two sets of steps and a path lead down to Bay Road. Turn left, pass under a huge brick arch below the bridge, and follow the road down through a housing estate to Wormit Bay.

Elie to Lower Largo

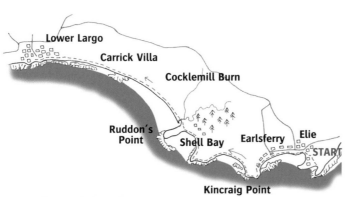

Lower Largo
Carrick Villa
Cocklemill Burn
Ruddon's Point
Shell Bay
Earlsferry
Elie
START
Kincraig Point

The seaside villages of Elie and Earlsferry stand shoulder to shoulder on the southern-most tip of Fife's pretty East Neuk. Since the first Victorian holidaymakers travelled here back in the 19th century, the area's unique character has ensnared many generations.

From the car park, follow the access track inland and, where it joins the public road, turn left, down to Harbour Road. Turn right on to Stenton Road and follow this to the High Street. Head east along the main thoroughfare, passing a church, and then on along Bank Street and Links Place to **Earlsferry High Street**, which leads down to a golf course.

The community, which was founded as a Royal burgh in 1223, is so called because the Earl of MacDuff was ferried across the Forth here by fishermen as he fled from MacBeth.

Go straight on past a small parking area and a narrow lane curves south by a row of cottages, terminating in a turning circle. Head out across the grass to the ruins of a small chapel where there are wonderful views over the Forth estuary.

The path runs round the point, rising over a ridge of rock forming a natural wall to emerge on to dunes lying between a sandy beach and the golf links. It skirts round the back of the bay and, at the far end, steps set into the grassy slope climb on to the headland where there's an old wartime ruin. A narrow cliff-top path skirts left to a trig point below an aerial and telephone mast. There are more concrete wartime structures here in the form of cylindrical pits, which used to house large guns.

The path continues round **Kincraig Point** and there are vistas to the Bass Rock and Isle of May. Look back and

Earlsferry and **Elie** can be seen. Carry on and the way drops to some more military ruins, then curves right with the coastline, following the edge of an open field, before dropping by way of a set of steps to a lower path. This curves round the point to the caravan park at **Shell Bay**.

Bear left and follow the surfaced road west along the edge of the site. Remain on the outer road, keeping the dunes to your left, until the road swings right at the far end of the park. Leave it at this point and head west along a sandy track leading through a gap in woodland to the mouth of the **Cocklemill Burn**. Wooden bridges span the wide, marshy outflow and, once across, turn left and a path runs through the dunes to the beach.

You will pass more wartime ruins as you head along the beach. Carry straight on until you reach the wide outflow of a stream below **Carrick Villa**. Head inland at this point, over the dunes, to a small parking area and climb wooden steps to join the trackbed of the former Fife coast railway. The old line skirts by a prominent ruin, leading straight into **Lower Largo**.

7 miles/11km
Moderate, full day walk
Low level coastal route suitable for adults and older children. Care must be taken while walking on Kincraig Point as there are steep drops over the cliffs. A regular bus service operates between Lower Largo and Elie for the return journey. Check times before leaving.

Map: OS Landranger, sheet 59.

Start/Parking: Ruby Bay public car park at East Links, Elie. GR: NT 497997.

Log on to this walk at:
www.walkscotland.com/route15

West Lomond

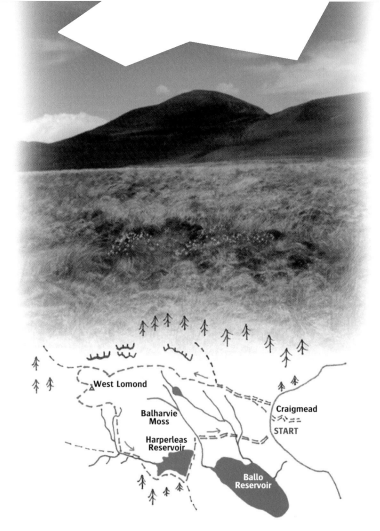

To southbound travellers on the M90 motorway the Lomond Hills bear an uncanny resemblance to a sleeping giant. Venture on to this slumbering form and you will find a landscape full of history. Below the summit of West Lomond is the deep ravine of Glen Vale where exiled ministers in the 17th century held secret meetings. As a result it became known as Covenanter's Glen. Above this is a craggy outcrop called the Devil's Burdens and legend has it that a local witch, Carlin Maggie, was turned to stone here after she dared to challenge Satan on the nearby Bishop Hill.

At **Craigmead**, follow the sign for **West Lomond**, the path starting at a kissing gate to the rear of the car park. The route takes you through some trees to a stile leading out onto the open grassy hillside. Bear left and climb up the gentle slope to meet a track hemmed in by two stone dykes.

Follow the track as it cuts a course through the heather. As you rise, excellent vistas open up to the north over the fertile Howe of Fife and the River Tay beyond.

As you reach the base of West Lomond, take the path to the right. The direct route from here to the top has been closed for a number of years to allow eroded vegetation to re-establish itself.

The wide grassy way soon offers views east over Loch Leven, a national nature reserve. Mary Queen of Scots was imprisoned on the northern island.

The summit is now just a short, steep climb away. The top of West Lomond is marked by a large cairn and, next to it, a trig point. To the east you can see her sister hill, East Lomond.

To continue the walk, pick up a small path on the south side of the summit. This steeply descends to a wall. Turn left and follow the wall east over open moor to a wooden stile. Cross the stile and descend to another one below. Don't cross this one, but follow the wall south to a third stile. Go over this one and walk east through a field of rough grass dotted with patches of cotton to a gate and, next to it, a bridge. Cross the bridge, where a gravel track skirts round the back of the trees to reach **Harperleas Reservoir**, part of Fife's public water supply.

Continue along the southern edge of the reservoir until you reach the dam and walk north across this.

On the other side a grassy path climbs behind the ruin of an old farmhouse to join a track. Follow this east as it runs around the hillside above **Ballo Reservoir** and finally emerges on to the public road a little way south of Craigmead. Turn left and follow the road the short distance north back to the car park.

6 miles/10km

Moderate, half day walk

A moderate walk through undulated countryside with short but steep ascent and descent of West Lomond summit. Suitable for fairly fit adults and older children. Dogs are not allowed within the perimeter of Harperleas Reservoir and there is sheep grazing on the moor.

Map: OS Landranger, sheet 58.

Start/Parking: Craigmead car park, two miles from the village of Falkland. GR: NO 227062.

Log on to this walk at:
www.walkscotland.com/route16

Crail to St Monans

The East Neuk village of Crail is perhaps best known for its picturesque harbour, a spot that draws artists in from around the country. It is also the starting point for this walk south along the Fife coast. The route follows part of the Fife Coastal Path and is a great introduction to a long distance walk that will link the Forth and Tay road bridges once complete.

From the harbour, head up to the centre of the village, turn left and follow the main street south to West Braes. Turn left into this narrow lane and walk out towards the coast. It curves right and then left along Osborne Place to meet the coastal path on the edge of the **Crail**. A wooden sign marks the start of this next stretch of coastal walk and a wide gravel path strikes out, dropping to a grassy bank above the foreshore.

The path is good but becomes dotted with rocks as you approach a boarded-up cottage at **The Pans**. The way crosses a wall and continues to Caipie Caves, said to have been a dwelling as far back as 2000BC.

The path goes on past a farm to reach Cellardyke. The approach is through Kilrenny Mills Caravan Park. Follow the road straight along The Cooperage, a narrow street of traditional East Neuk fishing cottages. Continue on Shore Street and then James Street and bear left when you reach the main road, following it round to **Anstruther** harbour.

A colourful array of fishing boats occupy this safe haven and the

Scottish Fisheries Museum, which opened in 1969, is well worth a visit. Exhibits are displayed within old cottages and boat-building sheds clustered around a courtyard. Wander along the harbourside and enjoy fish and chips or an ice-cream on one of the waterfront benches as you watch fishermen at work.

At the far end, before the main road curves right, drop down on to the beach and, a few yards further on, stepping stones take you across the Dreel Burn in the shadow of the town's kirk. At the top of a short flight of steps, turn right and head up to the main road. Walk south out of town, passing the Dreel Tavern, and take the next road on the left. Turn right in front of the primary school and Shore Road leads out to the local golf club. Beyond this the coastal path skirts a sandy beach with the next port of call, **Pittenweem**, looming into view.

Steps rise to the edge of the town and a grassy path runs between houses and the cliff top, emerging on to Abbey Wall Road. It curves left, descending to the busy fishing harbour. Mid Shore and East Shore take you on through a car park and a tarmac path that meanders along the front of a row of seafront cottages above the beach.

Walk on along the sand and the coastal path skirts by an outdoor

7.5 miles/12km
Moderate, full day walk
Well graded and well signed coastal path. This walk is a linear one and regular bus services link St Monans with Crail for the return journey. Remember to check bus times before leaving.

Map: OS Landranger, sheet 59.

Start/Parking: Crail harbour. GR: NO 612073. Plenty of on-street parking in Crail.

Log on to this walk at: www.walkscotland.com/route17

swimming pool. Continue to St Philip's windmill, an 18th century structure on the edge of **St Monans**.

The gravel path borders a park until it reaches a car park. Follow the road straight ahead to St Monans harbour.

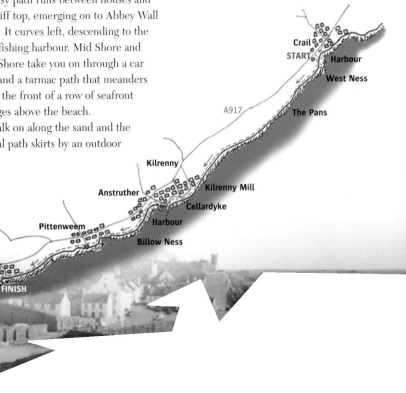

Ben Cleuch

At 2363 feet, or 721 metres, Ben Cleuch is the highest peak in the Ochils, a range of rolling hills stretching between Stirling and Glen Devon. It is an ideal introduction to the many walking possibilities in this often overlooked part of Scotland.

At the entrance to the car park, a wide path goes left through woodland. Where it forks a short way on, take the right hand path and climb through the trees until it curves sharp right. Leave it at this point and go straight ahead on a path that crosses a narrow wooded gorge and burn.

On the other side, the way emerges on to open hillside at a kissing gate and joins a track. Bear right and follow this as it rises into the glen. The climb is initially strenuous as the route twists and turns up the slope but the gradient eases as the track straightens out and runs north towards **Ben Ever**.

Continue through a gate and, a short way on, at a second gate, a wide grassy path on the right leaves the main track and climbs over the hillside. Follow it as it rises through grass, passing a small sheep enclosure on the left.

Higher up, on the ridge, the way passes a small pool of water – the top of Ben Ever is just a short distance from here.

From the summit, the path drops to a wooden gate at the junction of three fences. Cross where the remains of an ageing wooden stile are to be found and climb to the right of the fence to reach the trig point on the top of **Ben Cleuch**.

This grassy lump may not be the most distinguished peak in Scotland, but it is an excellent viewpoint. To the south is the urban sprawl of industry clustered around the River Forth. However, look north and, on a good day, you should be able to see Ben Vorlich and Stuc a'Chroin in the distance and, beyond them, the pyramidal peaks of Ben More and Stob Binnein.

To descend, follow the path east from

the summit over **The Law**, a low top on the ridge above **Tillicoultry**. Beyond it, the path drops steeply to cross a bridge over the Gannel Burn at the top of **Mill Glen**.

On the other side, take the path on the left. This goes down the east side of the gorge, skirting the hillside and dropping over open ground to a small gate. Beyond this a path leads to a car park.

Follow the road a short way from the car park down the left side of the burn and turn right, crossing a footbridge over the stream. Walk along Scotland Place to a path at the end, which crosses a driveway and disappears into bushes to emerge on to a narrow surfaced road. A few yards to the right a green sign marks the start of a public footpath back to **Alva**. It runs alongside a golf course, into woodland and then emerges on to a road leading back to the car park.

![three boot icons]

6 miles/10km

Challenging, full day walk

A strenuous hike to the summit of the highest peak in the Ochils suitable for fit and fairly experienced hillwalkers and older children. Sheep grazing means dogs should be on the lead.

Maps: OS Landranger, sheet 58, Harvey's Ochil Hills

Start/Parking: Woodlands Park car park, Alva. GR: NS 898975. The car park is reached from the main A91, with the turn-off on the north side of the road on the eastern edge of Alva, signed for Farriers Hotel and craft shop.

Log on to this walk at:
www.walkscotland.com/route18

Dollar Glen

Lying in the shadow of the rolling Ochil Hills is Dollar Glen, a dark, leafy gorge almost rainforest-like in appearance. The fifteenth century Castle Campbell crowns the valley and below waterfalls tumble over moss-covered rocks. The walk rises through the glen and strikes out over open moor, providing a spectacular contrast to the early part of the route.

From the main street through **Dollar**, East and West Burnside run parallel either side of the **Dollar Burn** up to a narrow stone bridge in front of a museum. Between this and the golf clubhouse on the left, a narrow path continues up the burn to Mill Green. At the top end of the park, you will reach a stone cairn and information board.

Two paths go up the glen from here, one on either side of the burn. The route on the east side is officially closed due to an unsafe bridge which is a shame as it is the more interesting.

The west bank path crosses the burn by a substantial wooden footbridge and rises quite steeply at first, although there are steps carved in the hillside. It levels off and runs along the edge of a golf course, then drops into the valley below **Castle Campbell**.

The route emerges at the entrance to

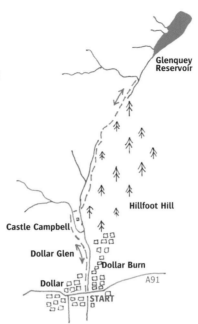

The castle is well worth a visit (there is an admission charge), particularly for the grandstand views from the manicured front lawn.

From the entrance gate, follow the access road north. It curves left and then right, crossing a stream at a shallow cobbled ford with a bridge. The route rises again, offering glimpses of the castle through the trees, then reaches a cottage at its high point. Leave the surfaced road here and turn left on to a track, signed 'Public Footpath to Glendevon'.

The way climbs gently through bracken on the lower slopes of **Hillfoot Hill**, then disappears into thick coniferous woodland at a wooden gate. Follow the track into the trees. A short way on, there is a three-way fork. Take the middle path, following a waymarker – a good path follows a break in the trees, eventually emerging on to moor at another gate.

The path skirts under looming crags and reaches its high point at the bottom tip of the forest. From here there's a wonderful view down the glen to **Glenquey Reservoir**. The path continues to Glendevon and makes a fine through walk, but for this route you should turn round and retrace your steps to Castle Campbell. When you rejoin the road above the castle, either go left and follow the road back into Dollar or return by the path in the glen.

5 miles/8km
Easy, half day walk
An easy route with paths throughout suitable for all ages and abilities. Take care in the glen, particularly with children and dogs, as there are some steep drops. Dogs should be on the lead both in Dollar Glen and on the hillside beyond (where there are sheep grazing).

Maps: OS Landranger, sheet 58, Harvey's Ochil Hills.

Start/Parking: The clock tower at the junction between East and West Burnside and the main street through Dollar. GR: NS 964979. There is plenty of parking in the town.

Log on to this walk at:
www.walkscotland.com/route19

Goatfell

Goatfell is a cracking wee hill, and a Corbett to boot. It is the highest point on Arran and the summit is a top spot for views across the island. There are various paths up the peak, one of the most popular being the tourist route from Brodick, the principal town on Arran. The Goatfell walk, however, starts further up the coast, approaching the hill from Glen Sannox.

The route leaves the road on its west side, next to a white cottage, and sets off up a track, passing through a gate. Following the river upstream, you will pass a tall white pole before reaching the first remnants of the old **Glen Sannox** mining industry – a roofless cottage and some concrete ruins. Stay with the track below mine workings and fenced off shafts to reach the river which you must wade or walk across. On the other side, the track narrows to a path.

The way is wet and muddy in places, increasingly so near the top of the glen. Here you must cross the water again then a well-constructed path climbs steeply on to **The Saddle**.

As you emerge on to the col, views open south down **Glen Rosa**, one of the approach routes to **Goatfell** from Brodick. The first top to conquer is **North Goatfell**, an easy climb. From the summit, walk south to Goatfell, half a mile away. A well graded ridge – **Stacach** – links the two peaks. On this section you can scramble over a set of delightful granite tors.

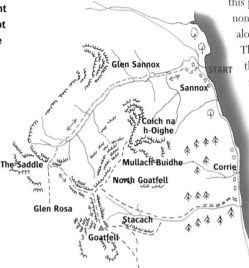

Alternatively, a path skirts to the left of the steep mounds.

Goatfell's trig point sits amid a crazy-paving of big slabs. A viewpoint indicator leads the eye to surrounding landmarks, including the coast of Ireland.

The easiest way to return to Sannox is via the path of ascent. An alternative for the more adventurous, however, is to retrace your steps north along the ridge towards North Goatfell, then follow the path beneath the summit to **Mullach Buidhe**, the top perched on the edge of the crags above Glen Sannox.

An obvious path continues north, leading to the crowning glory of the day's expedition,

Cioch na h-Oighe. The route out on to this peak involves a relatively easy, but none-the-less exhilarating, scramble along a narrow ridge of rocky teeth. This can be avoided by descending the spur on the south side of Coire na Ciche. The way narrows on the first of the rocky tors, and you must pick your way round and over huge boulders of granite.

The summit of Cioch na h-Oighe sits at the end of the ridge and from here a path continues down over the northern shoulder. The descent is steep and there are a couple of tricky points where you'll have to negotiate a route round or over large slabs of rock.

At the bottom, the path strikes north-east over grassland to rejoin the Glen Sannox track below the mine workings. Follow this back to the start

9 miles/14.4km

Challenging. full day walk

A challenging route for experienced hillwalkers and teenage children. There is a good path up Glen Sannox, although it is wet and muddy in places. The ascent on to The Saddle is steep. In winter Goatfell is a serious proposition and when the mountain is under snow, this is a route for experienced hillwalkers with crampons and ice-axes and the knowledge to use them.

Maps: OS Landranger, sheet 69, Harvey's Arran

Start/Parking: Layby with public telephone box and toilets just beyond the northern end of Sannox village. GR: NS 016455.

Log on to this walk at:
www.walkscotland.com/route20

Elgol to Camasunary

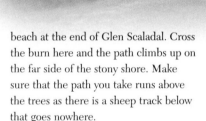

A coastal path leads from the scattered community of Elgol into the shadow of the jagged Cuillin peaks. It skirts the shore of Loch Scavaig, offering spectacular views of the famous mountain range. You can also spot the islands of Soay, Rum and Canna on a clear day. You'll need a head for heights for some sections where the path skirts above steep drops into the sea.

The route begins in the public car park in **Elgol**, just above the village pier. As the car park is part way down a steep road leading to the harbour the first stretch requires a strenuous climb up. Just as you start to run out of puff, a signpost for 'Garsbheinn' points down a track on the left. Follow this past a couple of cottages until it enters a gate into the garden of a house at the end, then branch off along a small path on the right, signed to Loch Coruisk. This leads out over grazing land high above the swirling sea.

The path drops to cross a burn then continues along the coast. The slope is steep in places with quite a drop below, but it flattens out as it descends to the

9 miles/14.4km
Moderate, full day walk
Low level coastal walk, returning via track and quiet country road. Take care on the coastal path as some sections are above steep drops. This is not a route for those who suffer from vertigo – a head for heights is needed in places.

Map: OS Landranger, sheet 32.

Start/Parking: Elgol car park. GR: NG 519137.

Log on to this walk at:
www.walkscotland.com/route21

beach at the end of Glen Scaladal. Cross the burn here and the path climbs up on the far side of the stony shore. Make sure that the path you take runs above the trees as there is a sheep track below that goes nowhere.

Proceed with caution and, if you have young children or a dog with you, make sure to keep them in check. The slope below becomes increasingly steep with a long drop. The path finally emerges into a grassy field where it crosses a stile and runs round to the beach at **Camasunary**. Walk along the sand, overshadowed by the craggy bulk of **Bla Bheinn**, and at the west end there's an open bothy – a great place to stop for lunch.

Back at the east end of the beach, below a house, a track crosses a bridge and rises up over the hillside. The climb is hard going. This route was built in 1968 by the army and while the going is rough underfoot, particularly at the top, the rest of the route to **Kilmarie** is well maintained and the walking is easy. From the highest point of the track, it's downhill most of the way to a hamlet where the track joins the **B8083** at a small car park.

Turn right and follow the road south. It is a quiet, single track route, but keep an eye out for traffic all the same. The

route climbs past a small cemetery and skirts round the western flank of Ben Meabost. Stay on the main road when it passes a turn-off on the left leading down to crofts at **Drinan**.

The road curves right and you soon reach the first in a series of scattered cottages on the edge of Elgol.

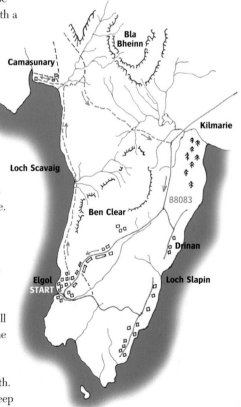

Raasay's Iron Brew

The beautiful island of Raasay lies off the east coast of Skye. This circuit round the southern end offers isolated moor and upland lochs plus some dramatic coastal scenery. You can also explore some relics of the island's iron mining history.

Set off from **Raasay** ferry pier and head up the trackbed of a disused railway line. Unlike traditional railways, this one was cable-hauled due to the steep grade of the incline. It climbs to the left of old mining buildings, passing a huge concrete hopper and kilns, but soon flattens out, and continues more gently to the ruin of an old motorhouse.

Cross a fence here and follow a narrow path through a break in the trees to an old viaduct. The concrete piers are all that remain and you must head down the steep bank into the base of the narrow little glen below. Climb out the opposite side and follow the course of the track until you emerge from the trees just short of more ruined mine buildings.

Tucked away in the foliage is a mine entrance, the access point to a grid formation of underground passages where the ore was extracted. This is one of Raasay's two iron mines. They were developed during the first years of the twentieth century and were linked by railways to the processing plant and loading pier at **Suisnish**. The mines operated through

the First World War, when German prisoners provided labour, but production ended in 1919.

From the tunnel opening, continue up alongside a fence separating the open moor from **Raasay Forest**, a commercial plantation. At the top end of this, the path crosses the **Inverarish Burn** and follows the stream through heather. The route is obvious for much of the way but it becomes less distinct as you near **Loch na Mna**. However, a couple of cairns offer guidance.

Carry on to the loch and follow the valley to the head of **Loch na Meilich**. It is worth making a short detour on to the summit of **Dun Caan**, a fascinating flat-topped hill shaped like a volcano. This is

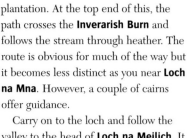

12 miles/19km

Challenging, full day walk

Open moor with path and track throughout, some of it a bit indistinct. Take great care around the mine buildings – they are less than solid – and don't be tempted to venture into the old mine.

Map: OS Landranger, sheet 32.

Start/Parking: Raasay ferry pier at Suisnish. GR: NG 555342. Leave your car in the ferry pier car park at Sconser on Skye. The Raasay ferry makes around seven crossings a day Monday to Saturday with no Sunday sailings.

Log on to this walk at:
www.walkscotland.com/route22

a prominent landmark, visible from the Scottish mainland.

Enjoy the excellent panoramas before returning to Loch na Meilich. Climb up a small stony ridge and begin the long descent, a path dropping to the single-track road. Turn left and follow the road south. After about a mile, it turns sharp right at a junction. Leave the road at this point and head south on the route leading past Raasay's tiny youth hostel. The way drops through Raasay Forest towards **Inverarish**.

Just before you reach the village, the route meets up with the main road. Turn left but, rather than going down into Inverarish at the next junction just a few yards on, follow the road east until you come to some concrete viaduct piers. By a bridge abutment on the right hand side of the road, there's a path leading through the trees and out on to the open hillside. A short way on is the motorhouse that you will have passed earlier. From here, retrace your steps to the ferry pier.

...ast across Skye

Strath Mor, a four mile long ... **between Loch Ainort and Loc**... **the narrowest strip of land b**... **north and south coast of the Isle of Skye. The coast-to-coast link forms part of an excellent circuit starting out from the tiny community of Luib, where traditional crofting cottages have been restored, and taking in Torrin across the island.**

As the burn running through **Luib** to **Loch Ainort** passes beneath the minor road, a grassy track strikes left. There's a metal gate and on one of the gateposts a small red arrow. Climb over the gate and follow the way as it rises behind the hamlet. A short way on pass through another gate and the track climbs round **Am Meall**, following a post and wire fence.

The track reaches a small milestone at its highest point and descends from here behind **Dunan** where the ruins of a church sit just below the way. Continue down towards **Strollamus** and the track goes through a gate and reaches an old stone bridge over the Allt Strollamus. Just before the track goes over the bridge, an obvious path branches right, crossing a small burn and rising through heather. Take this and begin the gentle climb through **An Slugan**. The path sticks to the right hand bank of the river all the way up. Continue up to the point where the Allt Strollamus and Allt na Teangaidh converge.

Above the junction of burns, a collapsed riverbank interrupts the route. Stay on the right bank and the path is soon picked up again. Follow it up to the col where a lonely metal gate sits on the moor. Here the way flattens out for a bit before descending through **Strath Beag** to **Torrin**, cutting a course over the hillside, this time to the left of the burn.

As the path approaches Torrin, it crosses a burn and, on the other side, there's a fenced area. Walk to the right of the fence, then diagonally over open grazing land to meet the road between a new house to the left and, a white house on the right, this is a former church and is marked by a cross on the OS map. Turn right and follow the road down on to the shores of **Loch Slapin**, passing an outdoor centre on your left. Walk north along the road to a bridge over the river at the head of the loch. Just before the bridge, a track branches right, leading to **Loch na Sguabaidh**. The path follows the east shore for a way before heading out over the moorland.

Continue on to the south end of Lochain Stratha Mhoir and, at this point, the path crosses the glen and runs along the west shore to the far end. It curves left round the hillside towards Luib. This next stretch is fairly boggy and remains so until the path reaches a post and wire fence. From the fence, descend to Luib and join the road beyond a ruined cottage on the left.

11 miles/17km
Challenging, full day walk
Track and path through remote glens with some easy ascent, suitable for fit walkers and older children. Underfoot conditions in Strath Mor can be marshy, particularly around Lochain Stratha Mhoir.

Map: OS Landranger, sheet 32.

Start/Parking: Luib, six miles north of Broadford on A850. GR: NG 565278. Park by the BT phonebox in Luib or on roadside nearby.

Log on to this walk at:
www.walksscotland.com/route23

Map labels: Loch Ainort, Luib, Arn Meall, START, A87, Glas Bheinn Mhor, Strath Mor, Beinn na Cro, Loch a Sguabaidh, B8083, Loch Slapin, Loch na Cairidh, Dunan, Strollamus, An Slugan, Strath Beag, Torrin

Invertote to Loch Cuithir

Walk into the shadow of the spectacular Trotternish Ridge on the remains of an old mineral railway running from the coast to a quarry below it. Although the line has long been closed, its route and a track running almost parallel make an easy, well graded, figure of eight circuit.

From the layby at Invertote, cross the road and follow the minor road up to **Lealt**, a small cluster of houses. Continue along the track to meet with the Lealt River a short distance on. The track and road run together towards the craggy bulk of the Trotternish Ridge up ahead. The trackbed of the old railway is up to your right, but is not easily seen initially.

The track and the line of the railway converge two and a half miles from the start. The two-foot gauge railway was built to transport stone from a quarry at **Loch Cuithir** to a loading quay and kiln at **Invertote Bay**. Opened in 1890, the track was relaid in 1906 but the line closed nine years later when most of the workers

went off to fight in the First World War. A small steam locomotive was employed to haul the wagons over the short distance. The ruined kiln remains at Invertote Bay and there's a spectacular waterfall nearby, offering an interesting detour at the end of the main walk.

Take the trackbed up to the left. An easy climb along the line leads to Loch Cuithir, a popular spot with local fishermen. Along the way you will pass the remains of some old bridges and, in places, there are rusty old bits of track. Just before you reach the loch there are a couple of small streams to negotiate – they are quite easy to jump over.

Loch Cuithir is in the shadow of the ridge, a dramatic landslip that has thrown up some stunning scenery.

Here you will meet up with the track. Follow this back down to the point where track and railway cross and then follow the line of the railway for the return.

A little way on it passes through a gate. Don't cross the gate but continue along the right-hand side of a fence running parallel with the course of the old railway. Doing this means you avoid having to tramp through some patches of bog.

The track rises gently over open moor, passing behind the cottages at Lealt. A little way further on it meets the minor road leading back to the layby.

It is possible to get down to Invertote Bay using a path that starts at a gate at the top of the layby. This leads out to a viewpoint before descending steeply over the grassy hillside. It skirts above the kiln, curving right, contouring round the slope to reach the burn. Upstream is the waterfall, a narrow path leading into the steep-sided gorge.

6 miles/10km
Easy, half day walk
Low-level walk along a good track and grassy railway trackbed. Suitable for all.

Maps: OS Landranger, sheet 23, Harvey's Skye, Storr & Trotternish.

Start/Parking: Layby at Invertote on the A855 Portree to Staffin road. GR: NG 516605.

Log on to this walk at:
www.walkscotland.com/route24

Lost Villages of Skye

Experience the remote wilderness of Skye with a hike across open moor to a long-abandoned coastal community. Few places feel more secluded than a deserted hamlet, where empty cottages lost in the landscape have an eerie presence. The crofting communities of Boreraig and Suisnish are two such places.

neighbouring Suisnish communities were victims of the brutal Highland Clearances during the mid-19th century. Families were moved from the land to make way for sheep and while some found new crofts on the island, often with very poor soil where it was difficult to eke a living, many were packed off on ships to start a new life in North America or Australia – if they survived the lengthy voyage.

Animals still graze the area, but the only signs of human habitation are the ruined cottages above the rocky foreshore.

The path swings right through the bracken and meanders through the sad reminders of what was once a thriving community.

The route then heads down to the shoreline and skirts below high cliffs where waterfalls fan out over the steep slabs of dark rock.

Below Carn Dearg, the path climbs from the beach to **Suisnish**, a handful of abandoned buildings standing above the point at Rubha Suisnish. Follow the fence above a large

10 miles/16km
Challenging, full day walk
A long but fairly straightforward walk with path and track throughout. Some sections can be wet and muddy underfoot and the route runs through remote country.

Map: OS Landranger, sheet 32.

Start/Parking: Ruined church and graveyard at Cill Chriosd on the B8083 two miles south of Broadford. GR: NG 617207.

Log on to this walk at:
www.walkscotland.com/route25

green barn and, beyond this, the route curves left to meet a track next to an empty red roofed cottage.

Continue north from here on the track, above **Loch Slapin**, with views across the water to Bla Bheinn and the Black Cuillin beyond. It passes a couple of deserted buildings and crosses several burns before turning inland beyond the grassy bay at Camus Malag. Join the single track B8083 road east of **Torrin** village and follow this past **Loch Cill Chriosd** to return to the start.

From the car park by the ruined church at **Cill Chriosd**, walk north on the main road to a track on the right. Follow this up to a large brick wall and shelter and bear left around the structure. Pick up a grassy path climbing through the bracken to a track running level across the hillside. Turn right and follow the track, the course of an old narrow gauge railway, to the remains of a marble quarry.

Skirt left and climb a grassy incline to more quarry workings above. Beyond these a track rises over moor to reach its high point at a rusty fence west of **Loch Lonachan**. The way runs above the Allt na Pairte, crossing more moor, before descending to **Loch Eishort** at **Boreraig**.

Occupied for centuries, this and the

Beinn Edra

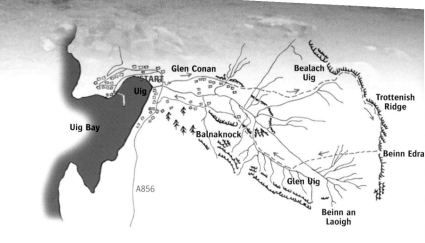

Stretching 20 miles north from Portree, the Trotternish peninsula has some of the finest scenery on Skye. It can be experienced first hand on this walk. The ascent, over gently sloping hillside, belies the true awe of the ridge, which only becomes apparent when you are right up on the craggy borderline between east and west.

Start in the village of **Uig**, one of the main ferry ports for the Outer Hebrides. Set off up **Glen Conon**, on the minor road that leaves the **A856** on the north side of the bridge over the River Conon, opposite a newsagent's. Initially the road climbs steeply, through several sharp curves, but eases off to rise more gently, passing by a strung-out collection of cottages.

It ends at the last house and from here a muddy track strikes ahead, passing over a stile. Continue across open moor, used for sheep and cattle grazing. There is plenty to see as you make your way up the glen. Particularly impressive are the spectacular waterfalls in the craggy amphitheatre to the right.

After about a mile of good track walking, the way disintegrates into an indistinct path that crosses a short marshy section. It reaches a fence running at right angles to the direction you are walking in.

Cross this and follow the fence down to a burn a few yards away, then pick up a path running alongside the water, following it upstream. On the horizon ahead you can see the **Trotternish Ridge**. As the path is quite vague here, aim straight for that point, climbing into **Bealach Uig**.

After a well-graded ascent over rough ground, you will reach the crest of the ridge – wonderful views open out across the east side of the Isle of Skye and the blue ocean. Turn right and follow the ridge up on to the summit of **Beinn Edra**, using a rusty fence to assist with navigation. The climb is not particularly steep, but great care should be taken and don't tread too close to the edge – the ground drops very steeply over sheer cliffs.

The summit is marked by a trig point, surrounded by a low, circular shelter of stones. From here you can take in the sheer spectacle of the Trotternish Ridge as it stretches south towards Skye's capital, Portree. There are also superb views west over Uig.

Descend south along the ridge, and follow the path as it bears right, heading west down into **Glen Uig**. The route follows the Lon an t-Sratha burn to the eastern terminus of a track, meeting it by a croft at **Balnaknock**. The track soon becomes a minor road, leading back into Uig. The final stretch drops steeply to join the A856. Once on the main road, turn right and follow it back to the start.

7.5 miles/12km
Moderate, full day walk
Minor roads, track and path over open hillside. Care should be taken on the ridge, particularly with children and dogs, as there is a steep drop to the east. Sheep and cattle grazing means dogs should be on the lead.

Maps: OS Landranger, sheet 23, Harvey's Skye, Storr and Trotternish

Start/Parking: Junction of A856 and minor road up Glen Conon. GR: NG 398639. Park in a small layby a short way from the start, by junction of A855 road to Staffin.

Log on to this walk at:
www.walkscotland.com/route26

Port Askaig to Bunnahabhain

Venture west from the Scottish mainland and a two-hour ferry crossing delivers you on to the magical island of Islay. Arrive at Port Askaig and the pier is the starting point for this low level route. Head north along quiet country roads and the hamlet that is home to the famous Bunnahabhain malt whisky is the next port of call.

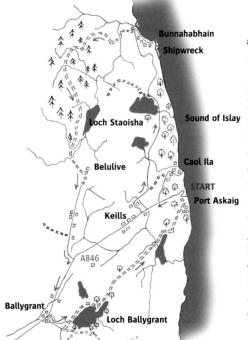

From **Port Askaig**, the walk begins with a strenuous pull up the **A846** as it rises steeply from the harbour, gaining height by way of two tight hairpin bends. Continue to climb as the road straightens out and follow it past a lane on the right leading to **Caol Ila**. Walk towards **Keills** but, just before the village, take the road to **Bunnahabhain** on the right.

The quiet single-track route rises to a steading at Persabus where it turns sharp right and climbs over open country. Stay with the road past Loch nam Ban and Ardnahoe Loch to reach Bunnahabhain,

a tiny village on the coast, dominated by its distillery.

The wreck of the **Wyre Majestic** lies out on the headland at Rubha a'Mhill. To reach it, follow the beach under the pier and continue to the far end. Pick up a path by a row of cottages and this leads round the coast to the boat. Retrace your steps to the distillery and go back up the road. Just beyond a hairpin bend, a track bears right, heading west over open land. It curves left and then right crossing the Abhainn Araig. The track rises to the edge of a forest.

A high gate leading into the plantation is frequently locked so you may have to climb it. Once over, the track rises through the trees to a boarded-up cottage and junction of tracks at Staoisha Eararach.

Head south, passing a ruined cottage at Staoisha and, a quarter of a mile further on, you reach the edge of the forest. Cross a ladder stile and the track spans two small burns before rising to a gate east of the croft at **Balulive**. The route bears right to avoid the steading and continues south, passing through a gate where the farm access track and public road meet. Continue south to the A846.

Turn right and follow the main road to **Ballygrant**. Leave the A846 on the

minor road opposite the Post Office and head past several houses and a quarry to a driveway on the left, leading to Lossit Lodge. Follow this until you reach a track on the left and let this lead you into the trees. There is another junction at the west end of **Loch Ballygrant**. Turn left here and the track skirts along the north side of the water, continuing through a band of trees to Loch Allan.

The track curves round the north end of the loch and climbs to a gate. Continue through this and, when you reach the high point, the way will descend to join the Dunlossit House driveway. Turn left and, beyond a gatehouse, rejoin the A846 just above Port Askaig.

14 miles/22km
Moderate, full day walk
A long low level walk following quiet island roads and tracks. Suitable for fairly fit adults and older children. Keep dogs on lead in places due to sheep grazing.

Map: OS Landranger, sheet 60 or 61.

Start/Parking: Pier at Port Askaig. GR: NR 432693. Public car park behind Post Office.

Log on to this walk at:
www.walkscotland.com/route27

A Sip of Rum

For decades the west coast island of Rum was known as the 'forbidden isle', closed to all except its rich laird and his friends. Now, however, it's a nature reserve and a walkers' paradise. The largest of the Small Isles, it has been a National Nature Reserve for over 40 years and is home to thriving herds of red deer, the white-tailed sea eagle, otters, seals and an array of birdlife.

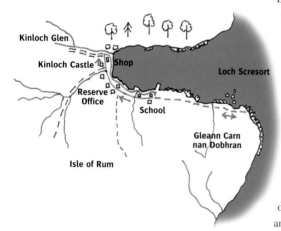

From the pier, walk west along a track to the island school and, from here, a path heads east through trees, emerging on to open moor where a black arrow points the way. The ground cover is mainly heather, boasting a delightful purple carpet during the summer. A short way on you will reach more woodland. The trees here were planted in the early part of the 20th century to provide shelter for game birds. There's a small headstone, erected in 1920 to mark the grave of a

local man who drowned after falling from his fishing boat.

The path crosses the burn in **Gleann Carn nan Dobhran** and continues to the end of the nature trail, at an abandoned village. From here retrace your steps along the coastal path to the school and follow the track west as it curves round the front of the building to meet a junction leading down to the old slipway. Don't take this but stay on the main track through peaceful woodland. The way crosses a burn and skirts behind a cottage. You will cross another burn a short way on before the track passes through white wooden gates. Beyond these it reaches the **reserve office** where there's a wooden shelter with information boards and a chart with details of conservation work and animal and bird sightings.

Carry on along the 'high road', following a sign for **Kinloch Castle**. The track passes two white houses and crosses a stone bridge to reach the mansion, built in 1900 by Sir George Bullough, a wealthy English industrialist. Its main rooms have been preserved and still contain the many unique items he gathered on his travels.

In 1957 his widow sold the island to the nation and it is now in the care of Scottish Natural Heritage. Guided tours

of the house are available.

Cross the main drive in front of the house and, at the next junction just before the bridge over the Kinloch River, turn right. The track leads down to a Post Office and small **shop**. Follow the coastal track south. It curves inland to cross a burn then hugs the shore round the head of **Loch Scresort**, leading back to the reserve office. Turn left here and a track passes the island's campsite to reach a solid stone pier where a path rises through the heather to a boathouse at the head of the old slipway. Follow the track from here back to the ferry pier.

4.25 miles/7km
Easy, half day walk

Low level walk, path rough in places. Suitable for all.

Map: OS Landranger, sheet 39.

Start/Parking: Rum Pier. GR NG 411993. There's a daily ferry service (except Sundays) operated by Caledonian MacBrayne from Mallaig to Rum. Sailings on Mondays, Wednesdays, Fridays and Saturdays provide sufficient time on the island between arrival and departure. Free parking in Mallaig.

Log on to this walk at:
www.walkscotland.com/route28

Glen Callater

9 miles/14.4km
Moderate, full day walk
A level walk suitable for adults and older children. Remember that a river crossing must be made if you intend circumnavigating the loch. Take some provisions for a picnic at the bothy, but carry your rubbish home with you.

Maps: OS Landranger, sheet 43, Harvey's Lochnagar & Glen Shee.

Start/Parking: Auchallater on the A93, near Braemar. GR: NO 156883.

Log on to this walk at:
www.walkscotland.com/route29

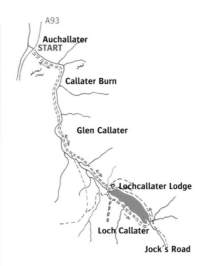

Discover a tranquil lochan with an excellent wee bothy on this route near the pretty town of Braemar. The walk starts at Auchallater, a cluster of farm buildings on the A93 south of Braemar where the road passes over the Callater Burn at a bridge.

The track is signposted as a right of way to Glen Doll via **Jock's Road** and passes through a gate before curving round the steep little knoll of Sron Dubh. It follows the bank of the **Callater Burn**, which tumbles merrily over a rocky bed producing many cascades and miniature waterfalls. After about two miles, the track crosses a wooden bridge and the burn curves off to the right and is quickly lost to view. Another half a mile or so of level walking brings a junction, the right fork climbing up the Bealach Buidhe towards Carn Dubh, the left meeting again with the burn (on the opposite bank now) and eventually the stout little **Lochcallater Lodge** and neighbouring Callater Stables bothy.

This delightful open shelter, maintained by the Mountain Bothies Association, makes a perfect place to stop for a brew. Linger here in summer and you may well be greeted by inquisitive wagtails, who creep ever closer in the hope of picking up a crumb or two.

To make a circuit of the loch, head southwest past the lodge and cross the burn at a bridge before picking up the track which cuts along the south shore. The way undulates gently as it hugs the lochside but no real effort is required for this. At the end of **Loch Callater** the path thins out and become ever more indistinct as it passes through some muddy reed beds. To gain the path on the opposite side of the valley you must cross the Allt an Loch. In summer this presents no real difficulty and if you are wearing boots and gaiters it is highly likely that you can run the burn without getting your socks wet. A good spot to do this is at the point where the tiny Allt a Chlaiginn joins the confluence.

The narrow path on this northern side is strictly single file and can be quite muddy in places. Take care on certain sections where it runs close to the edge of the loch. As you near the lodge you'll pass a couple of fine shingle beaches. There is also a large pyramid-shaped rock at the water's edge, a good photo stop with the cliffs of Creag Leachdach and Tolmount in the background.

Climb over a grassy slope, negotiate a stile in the fence and cross the burn to reach the lodge and bothy. Simply retrace your steps back home down **Glen Callater** with the Cairngorms and Morrone dominating the skyline ahead.

Loch Muick

Loch Muick occupies a dark, steep-sided glen on the Royal family's Balmoral estate. This route offers a gentle lochside circuit, plus an optional detour to a stunning waterfall with breathtaking views over Loch Muick. There is also a bad weather alternative should you arrive at Spittal of Glenmuick hoping for a day on Lochnagar, only to find the elements conspiring against you.

Set off from the public car park at the Spittal, located at the end of the public road in from Ballater. The track extends from the end of the surfaced road down over a bridge and passes a picnic area and public toilets to reach a small ranger centre, housing an exhibition of local flora and fauna. The displays give a pointer to some of the wildlife you can hope to see along the way. Red deer are among the more common attractions, while other less common creatures to look out for include red squirrels, ptarmigan and various birds of prey. At a barrier gate just beyond the ranger centre, keep going straight ahead, following a wooden sign for the **Loch Muick** (pronounced 'mick') circuit. Continue along this route and avoid taking a track on the left signed for the **Capel Mounth**.

A little way beyond this junction, a wide path branches off to the right and descends to a wooden footbridge over the River Muick. Cross and walk round the north end of the loch to a stone boathouse on the far side. A path connects up with a good track that you should follow south down the lochside. The route runs along slightly up from the water and there are excellent views down the glen.

In due course you will reach forestry surrounding the lodge at Glas-allt-Shiel. Just inside the woodland, a path leaves the track on the right and rises gently through tall Scots Pine trees to a bridge over the burn. Immediately behind the lodge, which is a popular summer picnic spot for the Royal family, a path climbs steeply up the hillside. Take this if you want to make the short detour to a spectacular **waterfall**. The climb is hard going but it's more than made up for by the stunning views you will see when you get there.

Otherwise, continue round the back of the lodge to rejoin the lochside track. Follow it round the head of the loch, crossing the two fingers of the Allt an Dubh Loch by way of a pair of low footbridges. On the far side, the track curves left and begins the return journey. The steep path that climbs up the hillside on the right at this point is known as the Streak of Lightning and when you see it the reason for the name becomes obvious. Thankfully you don't have to take this!

Set off on the lochside track – a third of the way along the path curves right into a little glen where it meets up with a more substantial track leading back to **Spittal of Glenmuick**.

7 miles/11km
Easy, full day walk
An easy, low level track and path walk suitable for all ages and abilities. The estate requests that dogs are kept on the lead.

Maps: OS Landranger, sheet 44, Harvey's Lochnagar and Glen Shee.

Start/Parking: Spittal of Glenmuick. GR: NO 310853. A parking charge is made.

Log on to this walk at:
www.walkscotland.com/route30

River North Esk

This walk spans the boundary between Angus and Aberdeenshire and, as it does so, it swaps the gentle flow of the River North Esk meandering gracefully through the trees at Edzell for the more dramatic torrents that lurk just a short distance upstream. There are waterfalls and deep pools to see, and on the way back, there's a chance to test the wobble on the aptly named Shakkin' Brig.

Start at the Post Office on the main street of **Edzell**. On the corner there's a sign for the riverside and **Shakkin' Brig**. Follow the lane down between the Post Office and a garage to a quiet waterside picnic spot.

Turn left and a path heads north along the riverbank to reach the bridge. Don't cross – save this treat until the end of the day. Continue instead on the west bank of the river. The path runs by the side of a field before entering beech trees. There are occasional benches should you wish to stop for a rest.

At this point the river is wide and tranquil. However, as you progress upstream, it becomes increasingly turbulent as the flow is squeezed between craggy steep-sided banks.

The path rises gently as the drop to the right increases in height and fences have been provided to keep walkers safe. A lively little waterfall is crossed just before the path meets the B966 at **Gannochy Bridge**. Turn right and cross the bridge. Leave the road on the other side and pass through a wooden door in the wall on the left. Beyond it, a path heads north, the river now down to the left. The woodland is again predominantly beech, although Scots Pine, oak and rowan provide some contrast.

The river is wilder than before as the channel narrows between rocks, cascading white water rapids crashing into oil-black pools. The path skirts below a big house up to the right

(**The Burn**) and passes above waterfalls, deep gorges and jagged rocky cliffs, all creating a spectacularly noisy and exciting atmosphere.

As it approaches the Pools of Solitude, the path climbs to meet the **Glen Esk Road**. The time has come to return to Gannochy Bridge. You can do this either by retracing your steps on the riverside path, or by following the road south.

At Gannochy Bridge, stay on the east side of the river and pick up a narrow path that leaves the road next to the bridge at a telegraph pole. This heads south on the opposite bank to the path followed earlier in the day.

The way rises to the ruin of an old sandstone building before broadening and continuing through a strip of beech woodland separating the river and open fields.

Further on the path narrows and

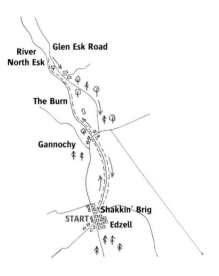

descends to the river. It is rough in places as it negotiates a maze of tree roots, and care should be taken. However, it quickly broadens out to reach the Shakkin' Brig. Cross and retrace your steps to Edzell.

6 miles/10km
Easy, half day walk

A well graded riverside walk suitable for all ages and abilities. Take care on the riverside path, particularly with younger children, as there are some steep drops, although fences have been provided. The way can be muddy in places, particularly north of Gannochy Bridge. Dogs should be kept under close control, preferably on the lead, north of Gannochy Bridge, at the request of the landowner.

Maps: OS Landranger, sheet 44,45.

Start/Parking: Post Office, Main Street, Edzell. GR: NO 602690. There is plenty of on-street parking, or use one of the two public car parks at the north end of the town.

Log on to this walk at:
www.walkscotland.com/route31

Roman around on Bennachie

Just west of Inverurie lies the well-known hill of Bennachie, famous for the prominent summit known as the Mither Tap. The hill is really a series of tops set out along a sprawling five ridges and although Oxen Craig is the highest point at 528 metres, the Mither Tap is without doubt its crowning glory. The Mither Tap is a tor, composed of a coarse granite and red felspar. In addition, an ancient fort with walls runs round the bottom of the tor. Bennachie is a place with much to commend it.

From the B9002, follow signs leading to the Back of Bennachie car park. Car parking is plentiful and there is an information board giving details of the various forest walks in the area. The summit trail is marked with orange waymarkers so navigation on this hill is unlikely to be much of a problem even for the inexperienced hiker.

The track sets off through the woods and climbs steadily alongside a charming little stream. After 10 minutes or so you will leave the forest, where the route strikes up the steep heathery slopes towards Little Oxen Craig and an abandoned quarry.

The excellent path towards **Oxen Craig** allows you to make good time and pressing on will see you at the summit indicator within half an hour of leaving your car. There is a cairn to complement the indicator but with the **Mither Tap** beckoning, you probably won't hang around here too long.

An obvious track leads off across the plateau in an easterly direction towards the edifice that, at 518 metres, is just 10 metres shy of its bigger sister. The large fort on the eastern face of the tor is hugely significant in terms of the area's history. At around the start of the first millennium AD the Romans forced their way north into this part of the country and evidence

of Roman presence in the area was found in 1975 at nearby Logie Durno when a 140-acre camp was discovered. It has been suggested that the northern slopes of Bennachie was the Mons Graupius, where the Britons were crushed by the Roman legions, and that the name is the root of the modern term for the region – Grampian.

Give yourself plenty of time to explore the exposed summit before setting off for the day's final peak. **Craigshannoch** lies to the north-west and is reached by retracing your steps from the Mither Tap and following the obvious path. From Craigshannoch rejoin the track for Oxen Craig and bear right at a junction that leads you to the main track just above Little Oxen Craig and the way home.

5 miles/8km
Moderate, half day walk
Steep initial climb is fairly tough but means that the hard work is done early in the day allowing you to enjoy a delightful ridge traverse. Good paths but this is an exposed area and it can be very windy on the summits. Suitable for fit adult walkers and teenage children with a head for heights.

Map: OS Landranger, sheet 32.

Start/Parking: Back of Bennachie car park off the B9002. GR: NJ 661244.

Log on to this walk at:
www.walkscotland.com/route32

Dunnottar Castle from Stonehaven

Launch an assault on the battle-scarred ruins of Dunnottar Castle, an impressive coastal fortress to the south of the Aberdeenshire harbour town of Stonehaven. The dramatic remains of the historic structure are just one of the highlights of this circular walk.

From the car park, walk along Beach Road which leads east to the sea and, once on the front, turn right and follow the wide pavement above the shore, heading south. Pass an amusement arcade and café and, a short way on, the local bowling green. Beyond this, the way crosses the Cowie Water. A concrete walkway runs south between the beach and the houses of **Stonehaven**.

The next river to cross is the Carron Water and a wooden footbridge spans the flow. Once over, the path curves left round the top of the beach to the **harbour**. Just before you reach the public car park here, a bend on the right leads through to the harbourside, emerging on to the Old Pier. A few yards left is Stonehaven's oldest building, the Tolbooth. This was once a store for the castle and it now houses a fascinating little museum.

Walk anti-clockwise round the harbour, passing the Marine Hotel and Ship Inn. Look for Wallace Wynd on the right and, when you find it, walk through this

narrow pend to meet Castle Street. Turn left and follow this to a steep path at the end that climbs to a minor road. Enjoy the excellent views over Stonehaven and the harbour, before turning left to follow the road up to a tight corner a few yards on. As the road banks right, a path branches left. This leads up towards a prominent memorial on the hillside, erected in memory of local men who died during the First World War.

Follow the path along the coast, passing through open fields. The impressive ruin of the castle looms into view long before you reach it.

The castle is well worth a visit. Built on a craggy lump of rock lashed by North Sea waves, cliffs below the walls of **Dunnottar** drop straight into the bubbling tidal cauldron. Over the years it has been the setting for angry sieges and bloody battles. In 1297 William Wallace burned a garrison of English soldiers within its walls and in 1685 160 Covenanters were imprisoned and tortured here. In more recent years, film director Franco Zeffirelli selected the castle as the setting for his movie Hamlet, starring Mel Gibson.

To continue the route, walk up the gravel driveway to a car park. Turn right and follow the minor road north. A

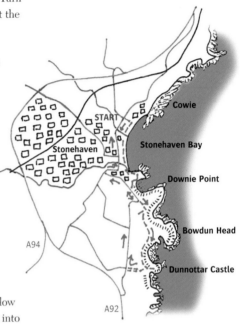

pavement runs beside open fields. The road passes to the left of the war memorial before curving right and then left. Continue on it down to the main A957. Follow the road into the heart of Stonehaven. At the square in the town centre go straight ahead along the B979 to finish at the Beach Road car park.

5 miles/8km
Easy, half day walk
Easy walk following seafront walkway, coastal path and pavement, suitable for all ages and abilities. Dogs should be on the lead over the coastal path between Stonehaven and Dunnottar Castle.

Map: OS Landranger, sheet 45.

Start/Parking: Public car park on Beach Road at north end of Stonehaven. GR: NO 875865.

Log on to this walk at:
www.walkscotland.com/route33

Clachnaben and Glen Dye

Clachnaben is an easy hill to identify from a distance. It is crowned by a prominent granite tor which can be seen from all directions as you approach. From atop this rocky protuberance, you can enjoy panoramic views over the fertile lands of the Mearns, to the sea beyond, and north into Deeside and the high peaks of the Grampian mountains.

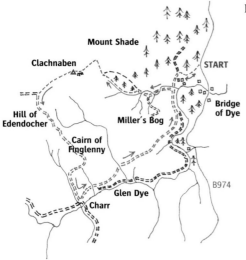

A wide path rises out of the car park through a peaceful mixed woodland, and there is a sign pointing the way. It descends to a rutted track less than half a mile on. Turn left and follow this down the edge of woodland.

The route crosses a lively wee burn and, at a junction of tracks a few yards beyond the bridge, turn right. The track follows the burn upstream, across the wide plain of moor known as **Miller's Bog**.

At the next junction, half a mile on from the bridge, carry straight on. The track rises gently to a gate at the start of a small plantation of pine carpeting the lower slopes of **Mount Shade**. From here, stay with the path as it skirts the southern edge of the woodland. The

stream remains close at hand, skipping down through a narrow leafy gorge to the left. Keep your eyes peeled for deer and red squirrels.

At the top of the woodland, a good path climbs into the col between **Clachnaben** and Mount Shade. It bears left as you reach higher ground and, with height gained, superb views open out over the surrounding landscape of rolling moor, quilted with deep green patches of forestry.

The path leads right to the summit of Clachnaben. Before you reach it a final haul will elevate you to the rocky granite tor crowning this peak. If you fancy a grandstand view from the top, the scramble up over the jumble of rounded rock is easy enough, but take care as there is a drop on all sides. The summit trig point is located a few yards west and a ring of stone encircling the pillar provides some handy shelter for a breather.

Head west along an obvious path which skirts through low peat hags to reach the top of neighbouring **Hill of Edendocher**. A cluster of high posts marks your arrival at a substantial track. Turn left and follow this south towards a prominent cairn capping the outlying shoulder. The track then descends to **Cairn of Finglenny** and, after a couple more rises followed by a final descent, leads to a cottage at **Charr** in **Glen Dye**.

At the junction behind the cottage, head east down the valley. The track skirts round the hillside to reach a junction above a pond half a mile on. Carry straight on. The route rises round the southern flank of Netty Hill before dropping to a junction. Go straight on, walking north to rejoin the track back to the car park at the bridge near Glendye Lodge which you passed on the outward leg.

10 miles/16km
Moderate, full day walk
An upland hike over good paths and tracks to the summit of Clachnaben, returning by Glen Dye. Suitable for fit adults and older children. There are sheep grazing at points along the route where dogs will have to go on the lead.

Map: OS Landranger, sheet 45.

Start/Parking: Small walkers' car park located 500 metres north of Glendye Lodge on the B974 Fettercairn to Banchory road. GR: NO 649867.

Log on to this walk at:
www.walkscotland.com/route34

Johnshaven to Inverbervie

5 miles/8km

Moderate, half day walk

A low level coastal walk suitable for all ages and abilities. This is a linear walk and there's a regular bus service for the return to Johnshaven. Check times before you go.

Map: OS Landranger, sheet 45.

Start/Parking: Johnshaven harbour. GR: NO 796670.

Log on to this walk at: www.walkscotland.com/route35

The charming coastal village of Johnshaven is the starting point for a gentle wander up the coast through old fishing communities to Inverbervie. Along the way, the route passes through the harbour town of Gourdon where an inn on the pier with a beer garden makes a pleasant spot for a midway break and some refreshment.

Set off from the harbour in **Johnshaven**, where a handful of small pleasure craft now take the place of the once thriving fishing fleet. There are still some working boats based here, but nothing on the scale seen during the heyday of the industry.

Head north-east along the shore road between neat cottages and sheds to emerge on to the coast at a small landscaped area of seating. Stay with the road as it leaves the village and passes by the front of a caravan park and, at the end of the asphalt, you will reach a wooden gate. Down to the right there are some pleasant strips of beach, ideal for a spot of sunbathing in the summer.

From here the track continues up the coast, running below the grounds of Lathallen School and then follows a high stone wall past a small encampment and, beyond this, open fields where the local farmer often keeps pigs.

After crossing a wooden footbridge over the burn at **Haughs Bay**, the path comes to a couple of seafront cottages at Haughs of Benholm. Carry straight on in front of these idyllically situated properties, following a wide grassy track. This runs between open fields on the left and a wide plain of scrubland, beyond which is a rocky beach, and then the sea. The main **A92** coast road is located on the hillside up to the left, but the rush of traffic is a world away and does not impede on the peace and quiet of the coast.

The track draws closer to the shoreline as you approach **Gourdon**. It skirts between the beach on one side and a row of cottages on the other to reach Gourdon harbour, another haven from the ocean now used predominantly by yachts, pleasure craft and small creel fishing boats. Like Johnshaven and many other towns on the Angus and Mearns coast, Gourdon was built on the fishing industry. Over the years the number of working boats has dwindled, with most of the North Sea catches now being landed in the larger north-east ports, like Peterhead and Fraserburgh. Johnshaven and Gourdon were unusual in that they originally employed line rather than net fishing techniques.

From the harbour, the route twists through a narrow street of cottages and sheds, passing below newer houses and a park to re-emerge into open country at Horse Crook Bay.

Follow the track round the coast to **Bervie Bay**, a mile on, and up the slope behind the sheltered cove, **Inverbervie**. From the bay, the road leads up to the town's main thoroughfare, spread out along the A92.

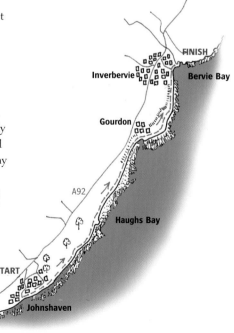

The Cairnwell, Carn Aosda & Carn a'Gheoidh

The Cairnwell and Carn Aosda are Scotland's two most accessible Munros. The two peaks sit within the Glenshee Ski Area and the Cairnwell summit can be reached by chairlift although to take such a route to the top would surely be cheating. At any rate, the peaks are easily conquered due to the high starting altitude and can be combined with a third, Carn a' Gheoidh.

operates during both the ski season and summer months.

A wide track rises north to the left of the **Carn Aosda** (917 metres) ski tow. The climb is strenuous but height is gained quickly and you will soon find yourself atop the stony summit that is marked by a large cairn. The views north over the Grampian mountains are excellent and on a clear day you can see for miles.

After you've caught your breath, head east down a track that runs around the top of another ski tow, descending towards **Loch Vrotachan**. A muddy crossing takes the path over a small burn in the pass above the lochan and up on to the long north shoulder of The Cairnwell. After a short climb alongside a fence a small path strikes off to the right.

This sets out through the heather and after negotiating a steep little dip, climbs up over a rocky knoll then runs along the crags towards Carn nan Sac, passing by two small lochans on the right. Wander out to a cairn at the end of the ridge for great views down to Spittal of Glenshee then take in the summit cairn.

A flat open moorland plain leads to the base of a short climb up on to the rocky summit of **Carn a' Gheoidh** (975 metres), the highest of the day's peaks. From the top, retrace your steps back towards Carn nan Sac and take the path that skirts left round to the two lochans and then makes its way back to the junction on the Cairnwell shoulder. The last ascent is fairly short but steep in places, particularly the final stretch from the top of the

7 miles/11km
Challenging, full day walk
A relatively straightforward expedition suitable for fit and experienced hillwalkers with good map-reading and compass skills, accompanying teenage children. The trio of summits is a good starting point for those who wish to extend their walking to Munro-bagging. Choose a good clear day for best results. In winter, when the mountains are under snow, this is a route for experienced hillwalkers with crampons and ice-axes and the knowledge to use them.

Maps: OS Landranger, sheet 43, Harvey's Lochnagar and Glen Shee.

Start/Parking: Glenshee Ski Area car park. GR: NO 138781.

Log on to this walk at:
www.walkscotland.com/route36

chairlift to the summit.

Homeward bound now. Return to the chairlift station and follow the fence round the top of the coire for a short way until the slope below eases off then descend towards the ski tows and retrace your steps to the ski centre and car park.

Leave your transport in the ski centre car park, cross the main **A93** road and pass along the front of the centre buildings. A track climbs steeply up behind them to a small round building – a café – at the base of a set of ski tows. During the winter the slopes hold the snow well and are busy with skiers. The weather is frequently bad and despite the relatively easy ascents involved, these are high mountains and require great care and the correct equipment. A chairlift runs to within a few yards of **The Cairnwell** summit (933 metres) and

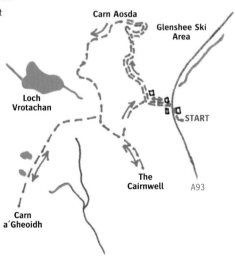

Carn an Tuirc, Cairn of Claise & Glas Maol

Glen Shee is best known for its sprawling ski centre but this area is also popular with walkers who can take advantage of a high level promenade to tick off a number of Munros in a single outing.

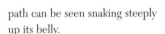

Instead of parking at the **ski centre** travel a little further along the **A93** towards Braemar and leave your transport near the bridge crossing the Cairnwell Burn. Below the car park, cross an old stone bridge and follow the path alongside the Allt a Gharbh-choire and soon you will arrive at a picturesque waterfall, which makes a lovely picnic spot in the summer. The track is boggy here and can become a little broken in places but the shapely peak of **Carn an Tuirc** (1019m) is dead ahead and the

9 miles/14.4km
Challenging, full day walk
A fairly steep ascent of Carn an Tuirc followed by a much easier high level traverse of two adjoining Munros. In summer the route should present no particular problems to fit adults with good map and compass skills and for accompanied teenage children. This is a good route for those who wish to extend their walking to Munro-bagging. In winter, however, it is a more serious proposition and when the mountains are under snow, this is a route for experienced hillwalkers with crampons and ice-axes and the knowledge to use them.

Maps: OS Landranger, sheet 43 or Harvey's Lochnagar and Glen Shee.

Start/Parking: Small car park just off the A93, two miles north of Glenshee Ski Area. GR: NO 149800.

Log on to this walk at:
www.walkscotland.com/route37

path can be seen snaking steeply up its belly.

With the flat, stony summit of Carn an Tuirc conquered, head across the plateau to a second stone marker a few hundred metres to the south east in order to avoid losing too much height in the traverse to **Cairn of Claise**, the second Munro on the agenda. The tramp towards this 1064 metre high peak is fairly featureless and unrelenting but it isn't steep and the views are spectacular with Lochnagar, Cairn Bannoch and Broad Cairn in the distance to your left.

A steady hike of around 30 minutes duration should see you approaching the stone dyke, which runs along the hill's summit ridge.

The track here is fairly easy to pick out, even under snow, and heads in a south westerly direction towards the obvious bulk of **Glas Maol** (1068m), the third Munro of the day. The track passes a wooden marker post with the almost vertical cliffs of Monega Hill to your left providing a startling alternative to the rounded hump ahead.

The path intercepts a line of old metal fence posts and these are easily followed

up a rising slope that also brings one of the wooden ski fences into view.

The summit itself is about half a kilometre past the top of the ski tow and marked by a triangulation pillar shielded behind a stone wall. An obvious route down is to trace the line of the Glas Maol ski tow and then follow the Allt Coire Fionn burn. It is worth noting that if you are following the left hand bank of the burn you will need to cross it at some point and take care while doing so.

The stream leads all the way down to join the Cairnwell Burn and there is a little metal bridge just a stone's throw from the car park.

Morrone

Rising south from Braemar, Morrone is a Corbett enjoying spectacular views over Deeside and the Grampian mountains. The name translates from the Gaelic as 'big nose' – a fairly apt description of this prominent peak's profile.

Set off from the car park at the top of Chapel Brae and head south-west along a track. A short way on, at a junction, turn left and follow the track south up into the Morrone Birkwood Nature Reserve, one of the finest examples of upland birchwood in Britain.

Pass a house on the left and climb through birch and juniper to a viewpoint where a plaque identifies surrounding hills.

Nearby a small cairn has information on the nature reserve and, to the left of this, there is a marker post with 'Morrone' etched on it. A path strikes out over open hillside, climbing to a deer fence. Rather than a gate or stile there's a wooden passageway through the fence that deer apparently cannot negotiate. Go through and the ascent proper

begins, the path rising to a line of cairns. The top is still a little way off but the cairns mark the start of a more gradual climb. There are excellent views north over **Braemar** to the high peaks of the Cairngorms.

As you gain height the heather thins out to reveal more stony ground and soon a large aerial mounted on the summit of **Morrone** looms into view. The top stands at 859 metres high and, in addition to the mast, there is a trig point and a large cairn.

Continue the walk from the summit by descending south on a wide track that drops into **Glen Clunie**. This meets a minor surfaced road on the floor of the valley, opposite Auchallater Farm. Turn left and walk north, the route following the Clunie Water towards **Braemar Golf Club**.

Just beyond the clubhouse, on the left-hand side of the road, there is a wooden marker post with a blue strip painted on it. Leave the road here, turn left and follow a path up towards several

static caravans perched on the hillside. Behind them, a stile crosses a fence and, once over this, you're back in woodland.

The path is indistinct through the trees but you should head diagonally right up to the top where a wooden gateway passes through a deer fence.

The path skirts round woodland, bringing you back to the viewpoint. From here, retrace your steps the short distance to the car park.

7 miles/11km
Challenging, half day walk
A tough climb to the summit of a Corbett. Track and path throughout with a mile and a half of the final section on a quiet country road. Dogs on lead through the golf course.

Maps: OS Landranger, sheet 43, Harvey's Lochnagar and Glen Shee.

Start/Parking: Public car park at the top of Chapel Brae, Braemar. GR: NO 143911.

Log on to this walk at:
www.walkscotland.com/route38

Lossiemouth to Burghead

The Moray Coast in the north-east of the country mixes long stretches of golden sand with dramatically craggy cliff top scenery. Seabirds fly overhead as the crashing Moray Firth laps at your feet, the waves dancing under the brightly painted boards of brave surfers. Every now and then the peace and quiet of the coast is dashed as modern military hardware breezes overhead, bound for the inland RAF Lossiemouth base. This walk can be undertaken at any time of the year on all but the roughest of days.

From the West Beach car park at **Lossiemouth**, a short concrete pathway leads down to the long sandy beach stretching off into the distance. When the tide is on its way out, the hard wet sand on the water's edge is ideal for walking on. There is a path through the dunes but this runs close to the golf course and users risk being hit by stray golf balls. Follow the beach west, crossing a couple of burns, keeping the white **lighthouse** up ahead in view.

The beach skirts round below the lighthouse and in the cliffs, beneath its foundations, deep caves have been carved by the sea. If the tide is out it is possible to stay on the beach. However, if the water is high, you may have to climb over the low headland on which the lighthouse and a small wartime look-out post sit.

From the lighthouse, continue along the beach. The next long stretch of golden sand ends at a rocky headland. Above, houses cling to the cliff top. Leave the beach and climb up the grassy slope to pick up a path along the next rocky strip of coast. Sandy coves,

quarries and caves line the route. Nearing **Hopeman**, the path passes the village golf course to emerge on to the main street that runs down from the B9040 to Hopeman's tiny fishing harbour. Once alive with boats fishing herring, it is now home to just a handful of craft.

From the harbour, wander up the main street and turn right along Duff Street. This stretches out in a straight line and at the end curves left into a cul-de-sac of new homes. Before it does so, a path goes off to the right, alongside the garden of the last house on the right. Follow this out over the open fields that sit above the cliffs. Nearing **Burghead**, the track meets a fence running at right angles. Turn left and follow a short strip of track up to the B9012 road on the top edge of town. Turn right and follow Fraser Road down into town. Burghead is a fishing port dating from the early 19th century.

Grain from the agricultural hinterland w shipped from here and Burghead is dominated vast United Distillers ma complex. The harbour is worth a visit as is the sw sandy beach to the south

8 miles/13km
Moderate, full day walk
Coastal beach and cliff path suitable for all ages and abilities. As with all coastal walks, take care on cliff paths.

Map: OS Landranger, sheet 28.

Start/Parking: West Beach car park, Lossiemouth. GR: NJ 226709.

Log on to this walk at:
www.walkscotland.com/route39

Portsoy to Cullen

FINISH

Moray Firth

Cullen

Sandend

A98

Portsoy

START

There are three main ingredients for the perfect coastal walk – breakers crashing over rugged rocks, long swathes of golden sand and picturesque little harbours. This route between Portsoy and Cullen has the lot, plus an historic cliff-top castle to explore. Set off from 17th century Portsoy harbour and within minutes you're in open country, enjoying fine views across the Moray Firth.
On the rocks below, seabirds dodge the rising tide, while butterflies flutter over the purple heather on higher ground.

Leave **Portsoy** harbour on Low Road – to the right of Shore Inn – and follow it to the next road junction. Turn right and head up the hill, past The Square. Go straight up Cullen Street and turn right on to Marine Terrace, following a sign for the swimming pool. The narrow roadway leads out to the coast and a path runs above the bracing open-air swimming pool. It meets a track that climbs by a white cottage to a junction.

Turn right and a grassy track leads to the coast, narrowing to become a path as it curves left past an old wartime look-out post. It continues around West Head, cutting a course through a thick carpet of heather and gorse. The path meets a fence, crosses a wooden gate

and continues to a gate at the top of a grassy track. Turn right and follow this to a wooden kissing gate. Beyond, steps lead down to a wartime bunker concealed in the dunes at the east end of a spectacular strip of golden beach. Head around the bay to **Sandend**, a tightly packed cluster of cottages perched above a tiny harbour. Join the road, turn right and, a few yards on, a coastal path walk sign guides you up a driveway to the left.

The track leads to Findlater Cottage but before the house is reached, cross a stile on the right. Negotiate a grassy strip of path to the next stile on the left, cross both this and a second stile a few yards on, and head through the field, following the fence to a concrete stile on the far side. The path climbs over open land, before crossing another grassy field.

A section along the top of the cliffs leads to Findlater Castle. It was built in 1455 by Sir Walter Ogilvy of Auchlevin to strengthen his coastal defences and the cliffs below the solid stone walls plunge straight into the sea, making enemy attack from the water extremely difficult. The well-preserved remains are just a short detour from the main path and an information board provides

plenty of historical detail.

From the castle, the path widens and skirts along the edge of a field, curving right and dropping to a secluded sandy beach. Steps lead round the bay to Logie Head and, if you're doing the walk in summer, keep an eye open for Red Admiral butterflies skipping over the heather and thistles. The path passes a deserted stone building before rounding the next headland to arrive in **Cullen**.

7.5 miles/12km
Moderate, full day walk
A coastal walk on path and track suitable for all reasonably fit walkers. Some sections can be overgrown and if you plan to wear shorts, pack a pair of over-trousers as nettles and thistles line the path on a couple of narrow sections. Keep dogs on the lead due to animal grazing.

Map: OS Landranger, sheet 29.

Start/Parking: Portsoy harbour. GR: NO 591665.

Log on to this walk at: www.walkscotland.com/route40

Borgie Forest

Located just a few miles inland from the rugged north coast of Scotland, Borgie Forest occupies a vast tract of wild country well off the beaten track. Houses are few and far between in this far-flung part of the world and it is possible to go all day without seeing another soul. This means there is more chance for those who do venture out to spot some of Scotland's more elusive wildlife. Badgers, for instance, are known to live in the area. Deer, pine marten and wildcat may also be seen, and the small pools within the forest are home to countless frogs.

Set off along the forest track, heading south from the car park. The track passes a white cottage in a clearing before disappearing back into the trees. After two miles, it emerges into the open, but continues to be accompanied by trees on the right. The way meets the **River Borgie** at a gate and cattle grid, and runs alongside the water to a wooden suspension bridge leading to a ruined cottage and stone wall enclosure.

Cross the bridge, walk along the front of the crumbling building and a track bears right, climbing to a gate in a fence. Go through and head over open moor to the edge of the forest plantation, skirting right to avoid a marshy area where peat is cut and dried to provide winter fuel.

Follow the edge of the forest south, climbing gently alongside a high post and wire fence. Underfoot, conditions are boggy in places and the web of heather and grass can be heavy with water after rain. There's a path, but it is indistinct.

Stay with the fence, pass two large wooden gates and continue to a wooden pedestrian gate near the top of the forest. Go through and follow a grassy track down through a break in the trees. When it meets a wider ride a few hundred yards down, turn right and follow this to cross a burn. Continue along the break, rising initially before descending to join a substantial forest track.

The track drops to cross a burn, just beyond a gate, and rises, curving over moor to the left and levelling off. Pass a small quarry-like area on the right and the next forest break on the right leads to quiet **Loch nan Ealachan**, well worth the short detour off the main route.

Back on the track, continue north. Eventually, the track reaches a wide junction. Carry straight on to a gate and cattle grid on the edge of the forest. Half a mile from this, the way meets the **A836**. Turn left and follow the road to **Borgie Bridge**. Carry on up the main road and, on the left, just beyond a white cottage, is the start of the forest track leading back to the car park.

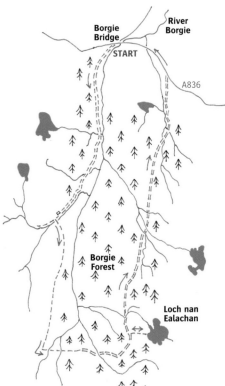

12 miles/19km

Challenging, full day walk

A long walk for fit adults and older children with forest tracks for much of the way. One lengthy section covers open moor where the grass and heather can be wet and gaiters are a good idea.

Map: OS Landranger, sheet 10.

Start/Parking: Forestry Commission Borgie Forest car park. GR: NC 664583.

Log on to this walk at:
www.walkscotland.com/route41

Stac Pollaidh

Stac Pollaidh – perhaps better known as Stack Polly – is one of those little peaks that it is very easy to fall in love with. It's never going to win any big mountain competition, but its charm lies in its dramatic elevation and stunning setting. Heading north from Ullapool in the car, Stac Pollaidh's unique form is easily spotted and few can resist becoming better acquainted with it.

The craggy little peak rises from the wild moor of **Inverpolly Forest** and resembles one of those ancient mountains you might expect to see in a film like *Jurassic Park*. A walkers' car park sits up from **Loch Lurgainn** and from here a well trod path rises over the hillside, straight up the south face, climbing increasingly steeply the higher it goes.

Our route, however, does not follow that direct and leg-sapping approach. Due to its popularity, **Stac Pollaidh** has suffered terribly from erosion over the years, but thankfully moves have been made to repair the original path around the eastern shoulder of the hill, in an effort to attract walkers away from the route up the south face. The project, carried out by the Footpath Trust, has ensured the removal of the worst sections of bog lower down and repairal of boot damage higher up. While much of the funding for the work came from agencies and organisations, a fair amount of money was donated by walkers keen to put something back into the mountain.

The path climbs from the car park to a junction about 400 metres up. Bear right here – the gradient eases slightly as it runs north-east on to the shoulder of Stac Pollaidh. It curves left higher up, flattening off to reach a junction where a steep path on the left zig-zags up into a col on the summit ridge. Take this and prepare for a steep pull up the slope. Once the crest is reached, there are breathtaking views over some of the wildest country in Britain. Panoramas extend east across the Inverpolly National Nature Reserve to Cul Mor and Fionaven in the distance. Canisp, Suilven and Quinag can all be seen clearly on a good day.

The highest part of the mountain – the western peak at 613 metres high – requires some exposed scrambling along the top of the ridge. Alternatively, a path winds through a series of spectacular turrets and pinnacles. The most difficult bit is called the mauvais-pas, a five-metre high rock step that requires scrambling experience. Although there are good hand holds, this should be left to experienced scramblers as there's a long drop below.

Better to simply enjoy the views from the ridge, surely the highlight of the day, before setting off down the hill. The easiest option is simply to retrace your steps round the eastern shoulder, back down to the car park.

Another option is to descend the northern slope to the foot of the zig-zag section and, rather than turning right to go round the eastern shoulder, head left, following a path that traverses the northern flank of the hill, beneath the west buttress. This descends through **Coire Gorm**, cairns keeping you on the right course, to the car park.

3 miles/5km
Moderate, half day walk
A short but strenuous ascent with the option of some exposed scrambling for experienced hillwalkers and teenage children.

Map: OS Landranger, sheet 15.

Start/Parking: Inverpolly Nature Reserve car park. GR: NC 108095.

Log on to this walk at:
www.walkscotland.com/route42

Sandw____

Bounded ____ ____ dunes and the crashing Atlantic waves, Sandwood Bay is a spectacular stretch of white sand in the far north. Its remoteness – the only way in is on foot – means that it remains wild and unspoiled. The estate was bought in April 1993 by the John Muir Trust, ensuring this wilderness state is preserved for future generations to enjoy.

Prior to the sale it was possible to drive up towards **Loch a'Mhuilinn**, but now a car park has been provided on the public road at **Blairmore**. From here, cross the road and set off up a track signed to **Sandwood**. Go through a gate and follow the way across open sheep grazing ground to **Loch na Gianimh**.

As you walk alongside the loch, keep an eye out to the left for a rock with a painted sign indicating the way to Cape Wrath.

At the east corner of the loch, the track reaches a junction. Turn left and it passes down between Loch na C____ and a smaller patch of water to your right. A good track continues north towards Loch a'Mhuilinn. This soon deteriorates and becomes a rather messy path, descending to the southern shore of the lochan. Follow the sandy beach counter-clockwise around the water and pick up the path again as it rises away from the lochan over open moor. Pass another couple of small lochans. Work has been undertaken here to rebuild the path, a victim of serious erosion.

The way reaches its high point above ruined **Sandwood Cottage**. Local lore has it that this crumbling structure is haunted by the ghost of an old mariner. The trust has carried out some restoration work to stabilise the roofless building, but there are no plans to rebuild it. Carry on down over the dunes to the bay where, at the south end, a spectacular stack called **Am Buachaille** – translated from Gaelic as 'the herdsman' – rises from the sea. The breakers on the beach make it a popular spot with surfers during the summer.

If you are just out for a short walk, your best bet is to enjoy time spent wandering along the beach before retracing your steps back to the start. For a longer, more arduous route head west along the sand and, at the far end, cross the river just up from its outflow. The stream is wide but fairly shallow

stony ____ ____ section is over rough ground with no real path. Head south-east along **Sandwood Loch** and continue through Strath Shinary to Strathan Bothy, an open shelter.

A bridge below the cottage spans the **Lon Mor** and an obvious path climbs out of the glen on the other side, rising

through low heather and grass to Loch Mor a'Chraisg. The path round the water remains obvious but becomes less distinct as it crosses a wide peat bog at the far end. Head towards a small grassy mound and then occasional fence posts keep you on the right track. A track is eventually joined, running down to join the public road. Turn right and walk back to Blairmore.

---

6 miles/10km

Easy, half day walk

A low level walk through wild and remote country with the option of extending the route to a harder circuit over some very rough terrain and a river crossing. Dogs are not allowed on the estate.

Map: OS Landranger, sheet 9.

Start/Parking: Blairmore. GR: NC 195601.

Log on to this walk at:
www.walkscotland.com/route43

Hill of Yarrows

Venture on to the heather-clad slopes of Hill of Yarrows and you'll find a land littered with archaeological sites. There are more than 80 known locations of interest here, ranging from simple burial cairns to more extensive forts. Many are well preserved and provide evidence of occupation dating back thousands of years. Our route takes in several sites and on the return leg, you can explore the Whaligoe Steps, a flight of 365 steps leading down to a small harbour. There is a story that for years these steps were maintained by a local woman who was convinced God, as a fisherman, would arrive at Whaligoe by sea and she wanted to be ready for him.

From the parking area at the south end of Loch Watenan, head back along the minor road for a few yards towards **Whaligoe** to Historic Scotland signs for Cairn o'Gets and Garrywhin. Cross a stile and take the path north over an open field, following a line of black and white marker posts.

At the other side of the field, cross another stile and head up over open hillside. The path runs across heather moor and over a wooden boardwalk, to reach the first of a series of chambered burial cairns. This has an information board outlining something of the history of the area.

From here, head west over a mossy dip on to **Warehouse Hill**. There is a vague path but you may end up making your own way through bracken and heather

onto the low top. Continue north to the next very prominent summit, marked by three large cairns. Again, there is no path and you'll have to battle with the heather.

This climb will definitely seem worthwhile when you come across the remnants of further burial cairns and see **Hill of Yarrows** in the distance. To reach it, head east over the open hillside, skirting round the west end of **Loch Warehouse** before the final short stretch of ascent to the trig point.

The summit of Hill of Yarrows is an excellent viewpoint with panoramas over the North Sea.

Descend north-east to pick up a track north of South Yarrows farm and walk along this to the end of the minor road (GR: ND 303443). Follow the quiet single-track road, which is dotted with small cottages and steadings, go east past Loch of Yarrows, part of the public water supply for Wick. Stay on the road until you reach a crossroads and turn right, following the road into Gansclet. When you reach the **A9**, turn left and follow it the short distance into the neighbouring community of **Thrumster**.

In Thrumster, turn right and follow a minor road east, past the Smiddy Inn on the left and the primary school on the right. When it splits, take the right fork, which curves south, running above **Loch Sarclet** to Mains of Ulbster Farm. Carry on past the farm

and head south-east overland towards the **Stack of Ulbster**. From there, bear right and walk along the top of the cliffs to Whaligoe. Emerge on to the A9 and follow the minor road opposite the telephone box back to the car park.

9 miles/14.5km
Moderate, full day walk
This route sets out over initially rough heather moorland, often without obvious paths where the walking can be hard work. The rest of the route is over quiet country roads and along the top of coastal cliffs where care should be taken, particularly with young children and dogs.

Map: OS Landranger, sheet 12.

Start/Parking: There is a small area of public car parking at the south end of Loch Watenan. To reach this, once in Whaligoe (seven miles south of Wick on A9), turn off the A9 opposite BT telephone box on minor road signed Cairn o'Get. GR: ND 318408.

Log on to this walk at:
www.walkscotland.com/route44

Loch Affric

Glen Affric is one of the most scenic parts of Scotland and contains some of the finest deer forests in the country. Lurking amid the craggy mountains is Loch Affric, a long blue ribbon of water surrounded by Scots Pine and birch woodland. The slopes on the south side are occupied by a Forestry Commission plantation, while the northern shores are part of Affric Estate, 9900 acres of Caledonian Pine Forest and open hillside. The area is extremely popular with walkers and tourists and when you discover the scenic beauty of Glen Affric for yourself, it is not hard to see why.

The public road in from Cannich ends at a Forestry Commission car park. Two tracks continue on although both are closed to unauthorised vehicles. Take the left hand one and walk down to a bridge over the River Affric, then pass through a high gate and strike out along the forest track.

A short way on, the track reaches a three-way junction. Take the right hand track and descend to follow the River Affric west. The track runs through heather, low shrubs and Scots Pine trees, passing a small lochan on the left. It then rises and falls gently as it skirts by **Affric Lodge**, across the water, and, after crossing the **Allt Garbh**, climbs round a small knoll before running along above the loch.

At the far end of **Loch Affric**, the track runs above a small strip of sandy beach with a wooden jetty before falling to a junction. Turn right here and follow another track by the river to a cluster of buildings at **Athnamulloch**. The way passes between a white cottage and a pair of stone sheds where there are boards with information on the estate. Cross the river at a bridge and the track rises past Strawberry Cottage, a former shepherd's bothy. It skirts round a low hill before striking a straight course west down **Glen Affric**.

Not far beyond Athnamulloch, a path branches off to the right at Cnoc Fada. Follow this north past **Loch Coulavie**, a picturesque and, in parts, reedy lochan which, like Loch Affric, is well stocked with trout. At this point there are excellent views down the loch. The way continues through the heather, crossing the Allt Coire Leachavie before flattening off to run along above Loch Affric, with a shore lined with gnarled Scots Pines.

As you approach the east end of the loch, Affric Lodge looms into view. It was built in 1864 by the first Lord Tweedmouth, a keen Victorian sportsman, on an island linked to the north shore by a causeway and to the south shore by a bridge. The lodge enjoys uninterrupted views for some 20 miles down the glen. The path drops to a shed then skirts along a high post and wire fence to meet up with a track at the entrance to the lodge. Follow this back to the start.

10 miles/16km
Moderate, full day walk
Forestry track and good path through woodland and over open moor. Suitable for adults and older children

Map: OS Landranger, sheet 25.

Start/Parking: Car park at the end of public road in Glen Affric, 12 miles from Cannich. GR: NH 200233.

Log on to this walk at:
www.walkscotland.com/route45

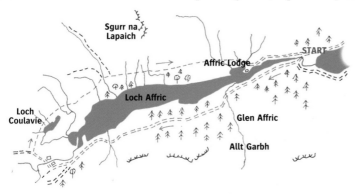

Lochan Fada

There's nothing like the tranquility of a mountain lochan on a calm day to soothe the soul; still waters stretching out from a deserted pebble beach, not a ripple in sight to disturb the moment. Lochan Fada is just such a spot. On a windless day the serene surface is motionless, a polished sheet of glass framed by the craggy mountainous backdrop of Wester Ross.

Pass through a kissing gate on the north side of the car park and turn left. Follow the path west alongside the fence to a small graveyard and then an outbuilding above a croft. Continue between the bracken-covered hillside on the right and grazing land on the left to a gate. Go through and the path leads to another gate then drops to cross a wooden footbridge.

Walk along close by the river, through pockets of woodland, until the path forks, the more obvious way going left while a grassy path bears right. Take the grassy path and continue below a waterfall to the southern end of **Loch Maree** where the path rises through oak, birch and alder.

The route crosses a burn in the trees and runs across open hillside to a bridge over the tumbling Abhainn an Fhasaigh. The path goes through a pair of metal posts and climbs to the right, rising alongside the river. It continues up through the glen with views opening out over Loch Maree as you gain height. The ascent is strenuous but the path good, although it can sometimes be wet underfoot. Up to the left is **Slioch**, a Munro.

Walk up to the highest point of the path where the way descends in a fairly indirect curve to cross a burn as it leaves **Lochan Fada**. Continue down to the burn crossing, the lochan in view below. There is no bridge where the path meets the burn, , just a series of rocks which can be used as stepping stones. Once safely over, a path skirts round the shore of the loch, passing several strips of beach before it rises over a headland to a longer beach. At the far end of this, you will reach a channel.

Cross this and the path bears right, climbing over open hillside above a smattering of small lochans in the base of the valley down to the right. It continues to gain height, passing the ruin of an old bothy, before undulating over the open hillside to eventually meet the top end of a solid track.

The track descends quite steeply to a bridge a mile below. Cross and, a short distance on, the way curves right to reach a junction by a stone shed and enclosure at **Heights of Kinlochewe**. Turn right and head south-west. The track passes a cottage and an abandoned house and, further on, meets the river beyond an open field and follows this across open grazing land. There are various waterfalls and pools to see as you follow the flow down the glen.

Continue on the track to **Incheril**. As you approach, the route rises to a new house. Skirt to the right behind the property to a gate at the top end of the car park.

13 miles/20km
Challenging, full day walk

A long and demanding walk following track and good paths through remote country. This route is suitable for fit walkers and teenage children. Sheep grazing over much of the route means dogs have to be under control. Stalking takes place on weekdays between September 15 and November 15 when the route is best avoided. If in doubt, check with the estate. Their telephone number is 01445 760207.

Maps: OS Landranger, sheet 19, Harvey's Torridon.

Start/Parking: Public car park at Incheril. GR: NH 037624. To reach the car park, the access road leaves the A832 on the east side of Kinlochewe. Follow the track straight through Incheril and the car park is at the very end.

Log on to this walk at:
www.walkscotland.com/route46

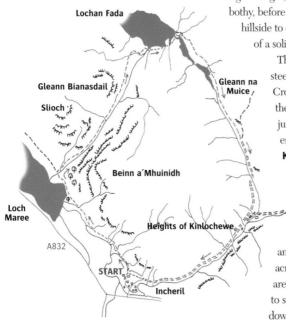

Loch Clair and Loch Coulin

The magnificent scenery of the Torridon mountains forms an impressive backdrop to this easy and picturesque track walk skirting along the shores of Loch Clair and round neighbouring Loch Coulin. The outward section follows the Coulin Pass, an historic right of way leading to Achnashallach. It was originally used by cattle drovers but is now popular with hikers keen to discover the many and varied delights of Torridon. Beinn Eighe is the most easterly of the Torridonian peaks and its long quartzite scree-covered flanks are clearly seen from the route.

From the layby on the **A896**, set off down the metalled road leading into the Coulin Estate, heading towards **Loch Clair**. Cross a bridge and follow the road as it runs alongside the loch. Stop every now and then to take in the impressive sight of Beinn Eighe behind you. At the end of Loch Clair, you arrive at a wooden bridge. Don't cross this but keep walking straight on, pass through a gate and below a waterfall on the left, and continue alongside a beautiful stretch of water. Depending on the time of year, the track is coloured by purple heather and rhododendron, and, up to the left, Scots Pine trees hug the craggy slope.

As you approach a second bridge, stay with the track, passing by the bridge. After a short distance, a path branches off to the right. Take this narrow, stony way (it is likely to be wet and muddy in places). The path climbs gently away, passing through a gate without a fence before descending towards **Loch Coulin**. Just before you reach the white cottage at **Torran-cuilinn**, the path is diverted round a small stand of scrawny trees. It then goes over a grassy field to reach a bridge. Cross the bridge and take the track as it bears right, heading towards the large white farmhouse at **Coulin**.

Follow the track round the left side of the building and continue north-west towards Loch Coulin. The route follows the shore in a north-west direction, to reach the bridge passed earlier. Cross over and a short path leads back to the track.

Turn left and retrace your steps to the start.

5 miles/8km
Easy, half day walk
Track and path walk suitable for all abilities at all times of the year.

Maps: OS Landranger, sheet 25, Harvey's Torridon.

Start/Parking: Small unofficial car park on the A896, three miles west of Kinlochewe. GR: NH 003582.

Log on to this walk at:
www.walkscotland.com/route47

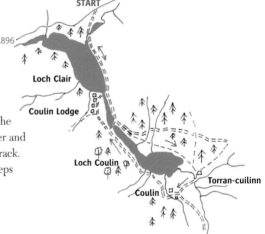

Falls of Foyers

The River Foyers drops 130 metres in the final mile of its journey from high on the Monadhliath Mountains to the shores of Loch Ness. Such a dramatic conclusion to its bubbling life does not go unnoticed, largely due to a pair of spectacular waterfalls linked by a very pleasant walk.

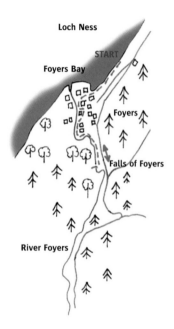

The road leads to a fish farm on the right and the old aluminium smelter, a substantial stone-built structure that appears to provide little more than an extensive storage facility now. In its heyday, during the early years of the 20th century, the plant – the first 'modern' factory in the Scottish Highlands – produced a sixth of the total world aluminium production.

Walk along the front of the building, crossing the tailrace where water used to provide electrical power was jettisoned into Loch Ness.

Further on, the road passes a small industrial unit to reach a junction. Turned left here and follow the road up as it curves left to reach another junction. Go left and the route reaches a health centre and houses above. Take the next track on the right, where a green sign points the way to the falls.

The track climbs by several houses towards a large white-washed property at the top. As you approach the entrance gates to this, a path leaves the track on the right, again signed for the falls. It enters woodland and skirts round above a steep drop plunging into the **River Foyers**, a bubbling cauldron of deep black pools and white water. Thankfully, there's a fairly new fence – the river is a long way down and the cliffs are pretty vertical!

The path meanders through the trees before climbing to an excellent viewpoint where the full spectacle of the Lower Falls of Foyers can be savoured. The way skirts left and hugs the slope as it rises from here towards the Upper Falls of Foyers. It joins the B852 above and this leads to a bridge over the higher waterfall.

Return to the start by retracing your steps to the pier car park.

Foyers Pier makes a good start for this woodland wander as there's plenty of free parking space. The route also offers a rather enjoyable hour or so on dry land if you're cruising the Caledonian Canal, or boating on **Loch Ness**.

To the north of the pier car park is a large hydro-electric power station. The current structure was built in 1975, but electricity has been generated here since 1896 when a tunnel was bored through the hillside to channel water down from Loch Mhor. This provided power for the former aluminium works located nearby.

Leave the car park and head south-west along a surfaced road lined on both sides by trees and heavy undergrowth.

2.5 miles/4km
Easy, short stroll
A short walk along minor roads and good woodland paths with some short stretches of strenuous ascent. Suitable for all ages, but take care as there are steep drops.

Maps: OS Landranger, sheet 26 and 34.

Start/Parking: Foyers Bay pier. GR: NH 502216.

Log on to this walk at:
www.walkscotland.com/route48

Caledonian Canal

One of Scotland's engineering marvels, the 60-mile long Caledonian Canal was created last century by Thomas Telford to provide boats with safe passage from one side of the country to the other. It cuts a course through the natural fault line of the Great Glen from Inverness to Fort William and incorporates four lochs in its route, including Loch Ness, home of the famous monster. There are 28 locks in total, lifting vessels from sea level at each end to over 30 metres above sea level at the highest point. Two can be seen in action at Dochgarroch, the start of this walk, where cruising yachts are frequently found negotiating the step.

From the small car park by the canal, cross the locks at **Dochgarroch** and head north on a wide grassy towpath running alongside the canal. The route follows a narrow island separating the canal on your left from the **River Ness** on the right. The river is concealed by shrubs and woodland here and it's easy to forget you are effectively walking a tightrope between the two.

On the opposite side, an assortment of vessels, large and small, line the canal. There are yachts, many with names clearly inspired by the great outdoors – *Ben Nevis* and *Glen Affric* among them – plus larger barges and boats.

The path runs below two pylon lines and continues north, by a boarded-up cottage on the opposite shore. Beyond another line of pylons, the ground opens out and the river becomes clearly visible. Continue on the towpath, ignoring a set of steps down to the right. In a short distance the most northerly point of the walk is reached, a swing bridge taking the **A82** over the canal. Cross the bridge and, on the far side, turn left and head south. Pass a small car park and the Jacobite Cruises booking office and continue between the canal and a golf course on the right. The way passes a shed belonging to the Inverness Rowing Club.

South of the shed, the path is sandwiched between the canal and a steep bank on the right. At the end of this you'll reach a black barrier gate and, beyond this, there is a cluster of houses. The path leaves the canal here and follows a track on the right up between a set of hedges. Head up to the next junction and bear left here, walking out along a track bordering woodland. Carry straight on, passing a path on the right and then a track on the left leading down to the boarded up cottage at Dunaincroy. At the end of the track, a path curves down, skirting woodland and gorse bushes, to rejoin the towpath coming in from the left at a stile. Go straight on and the way follows the canal past pontoons and a boat charter business shed to emerge at the Dochgarroch locks.

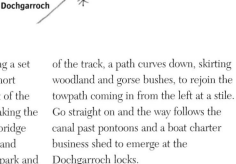

7 miles/12km
Easy, half day walk
An easy walk on flat canal towpath and woodland/farm tracks suitable for all ages and abilities. British Waterways request no swimming in the canal and, if you're taking a dog, don't let it foul the towpath.

Map: OS Landranger, sheet 60 or 61.

Start/Parking: Dochgarroch Locks. GR: NH 618405. There is a small car park by the canal. To reach it, leave the A82 at the Dochgarroch shop and follow a narrow road signed for a campsite.

Log on to this walk at:
www.walkscotland.com/route49

Kinlochleven to Loch Eilde Mor

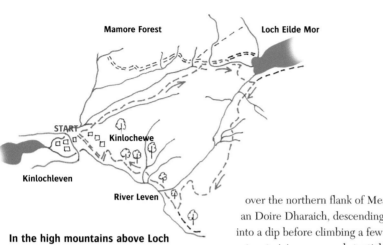

In the high mountains above Loch Leven lurks an enchanting stretch of water called Loch Eilde Mor. Translating from the Gaelic as 'big loch of the hind', the watery finger tickles the rocky underbelly of the Mamores, one of Scotland's most spectacular areas of mountain scenery.

At the back of the car park next to St Paul's Church in Wades Road, a path rises gently up through woodland into a clearing a short distance from the start, where it reaches a junction. Don't take the path on the left, but carry straight ahead, bearing right.

The way climbs above **Kinlochmore**, rising steadily at first but becoming increasingly steep as it begins to gain height. Down to the right, there's a stream cascading through a steep-sided gorge. The path runs through a mix of open ground and woodland before leaving the shelter of the trees for the last time a kilometre from Kinlochmore.

It continues to climb over open hillside, with views opening out west over **Kinlochleven** and Loch Leven. Above, to the left, is **Mamore Forest** and the magnificent peaks of the Mamores, a string of mountains stretching for over 10 miles in length. Wedged between Glen Nevis and Loch Leven, the range includes 11 Munros.

The gradient eases as the path skirts over the northern flank of Meall an Doire Dharaich, descending into a dip before climbing a few metres to join a more substantial track. A cairn marks the junction. Turn right here and follow the track down towards Loch Eilde Mor. Keep your eyes peeled for a path branching off on the right.

Follow this round the head of the loch to a dam over the Allt na h-Eilde.

Cross the dam and turn right. Walk along the path, passing two metal huts. Beyond the second hut, the path reaches a cairn marking the start of the descent towards the **River Leven**. Turn right at the cairn and a fairly steep path of grass and rock drops down the hillside. As it nears the base of the glen, the way enters woodland, reaching a gap in a stone wall next to a small stream.

A path rises from the wall to meet another path. Turn right and follow this down to a wooden footbridge over the Allt na h-Eilde. From here, the route runs through the trees back to Kinlochmore. It forks just before the village. Take the left arm and this joins the end of Wades Road close to the former aluminium smelter. Follow the road back to the car park.

9 miles/14km
Moderate, full day walk
Path and track throughout with a fairly steep climb through woodland. Suitable for fit walkers and teenage children. Dogs need to go on the lead in places due to sheep grazing.

Maps: OS Landranger, sheet 41, or Harvey's Ben Nevis.

Start/Parking: Free public car park next to St Paul's Church, Wades Road, Kinlochmore. GR: NN 187623.

Log on to this walk at:
www.walkscotland.com/route50

Blackwater Dam

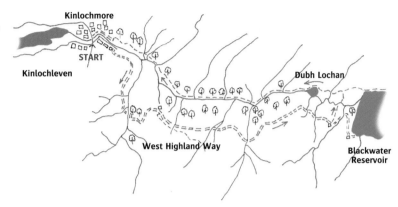

Kinlochleven owes its existence to the aluminium industry and the Blackwater Reservoir provided the necessary power. A smelter was constructed along with the reservoir dam and powerhouses between 1904 and 1909. The works has since closed but the site is being redeveloped with a mix of small business units and outdoor recreation facilities, including a climbing centre.

Set off from the public toilets by the main road bridge over the River Leven. The surfaced road quickly gives way to a track across the base of some huge black pipes. It rises steeply on the right hand side, following them up the hillside. You are now on the **West Highland Way** (WHW), on a track used to service the dam. The way rises steeply for a time before flattening out towards a bridge over the Allt Coire Mhorair, and, above it, a reservoir that provides **Kinlochleven** with its water supply.

Once over the bridge, be prepared for another gruelling uphill stint. A couple of tracks branch off on either side of our route, which is marked with WHW posts (a thistle in a hexagon). A small cluster of buildings marks the end of the uphill slog. Continue on the track past the cottages.

The Blackwater dam soon looms into view. It's an impressive sight, a giant wall of concrete stretching across the head of the glen. It is 3,112 feet long - just over a kilometre – and 86 feet high. When it was built it was the largest structure of its kind in Europe. The reservoir behind it draws water from 60 square miles of hillside with an average annual rainfall of over 100 inches.

The WHW branches off on the right and as you get nearer to the dam, a small graveyard can be seen down to the left. It was here that men and women who died in the massive construction project were buried. The headstones are simple slabs of concrete and while most have names, some are marked 'Not Known', such was the transient nature of the workforce that consisted largely of Scots labourers and Irish navvies. It is not possible to cross the dam itself, so the best course of action is to ford the outflow a little way downstream. At several points, particularly between two large pools, there are narrow channels and conveniently placed stepping stones.

Once safely across, head up over the grass and heather to join a well-made path descending from the north end of the dam towards **Dubh Lochan**. It

follows the River Leven down the glen and, to your left, there are beautiful little lochans and spectacular waterfalls, all lined with silver birch trees.

A substantial bridge spans the Allt na h-Eilde and, on the other side, the path disappears into woodland, emerging briefly before **Kinlochmore**. It skirts round the edge of the town and brings you out into a small housing estate. The streets all fan out from a central point where a pathway runs along the riverbank and brings you out by the road bridge over the Leven.

10 miles/16km

Moderate, full day walk

Track and path throughout, with the exception of a short point beneath the dam where a stream has to be forded and some agility is needed. There are some steep sections early on and this route is best suited for fit adults and older children. Dogs should be on the lead in places due to sheep grazing.

Map: OS Landranger, sheet 41.

Start/Parking: Public toilets, Kinlochleven. GR: NN 192620. Free car park opposite the nearby shops.

Log on to this walk at:
www.walkscotland.com/route51

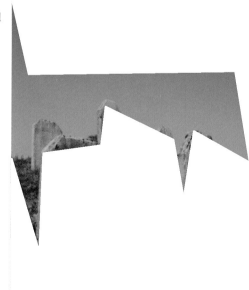

Loch Moidart and Castle Tioram

6 miles/10km

Moderate, half day walk

Path over open hillside and along lochside, rough and muddy in places. This route is suitable for all fairly fit walkers and capable children. Possibility of some cattle grazing on the open hillside so dogs may need to go on lead.

Map: OS Landranger, sheet 40.

Start/Parking: Track end at Blain, half a kilometre north of Shiel Bridge. GR: NM 677694. There is space for several cars on the roadside.

Log on to this walk at:
www.walkscotland.com/route52

Loch Moidart, just north of the Ardnamurchan peninsula, is one of Scotland's hidden gems. A shimmering finger of water hidden from view by dramatic mountains and protected from the rigours of the Atlantic ocean by a barrage of craggy islands. Its rocky shores are well worth seeking out and the best way to enjoy the peace and tranquillity of the area is on foot.

Just north of **Shiel Bridge**, a track leaves the A861 in **Blain** at a metal gate. Go through and the route climbs through woodland of beech, oak, silver birch and holly, a bushy carpet of rhododendron and bracken lining the wayside.

Continue up and a short way on a locked gate straddles the route. Cross at a stile and carry on along the track, bearing right to cross a burn before rising past a fenced enclosure. Leave the main path where it curves right and follow a grassy track. This leads into a small woodland of silver birch where it ends and a path continues, the way littered with stones. It is fairly muddy initially but improves as it gains height and emerges on to open hillside, climbing to **Loch Blain**.

The first clue to the lochan's existence is a small stone dam at its southern end. Beyond this the smooth lily-covered gloss stretches out to a stand of tall pine trees on the far bank. The path curves round the east shore, passing between Loch Blain and a smaller neighbouring pond. Follow the way up to the next junction, marked by a lone tree. Turn right and the path rises through bracken and heather to its highest point below **Beinn Bhreac**.

The path drops to the right of a cluster of ruined cottages. The lochside path is just a short way on. Keep your eyes peeled for the junction as it is easy to miss. The path, which goes left at the junction, meanders through woodland above **Loch Moidart**, offering plenty of opportunity to soak up the scenery.

As you head west, it drops on to an open rock ledge above the water. Take care on this stretch, particularly if you have younger children or a dog with you. A short way on from the ledge, the path curves left around the headland and **Castle Tioram** suddenly looms into view.

If the tide is low, the castle – built on an offshore island – can be reached on foot. Head across the grass and then over open beach separating the island on which the castle sits from the mainland. Climb the grassy path leading to the castle and you will find an entrance on the north side of the stone structure. Constructed in the 13th century to protect the area from attack, Castle Tioram witnessed centuries of clan battle before being gutted by fire in 1715. Take care to ensure, however, that the incoming tide does not leave you stranded on the island.

Set off from the castle car park and follow the single-track road south back to Blain.

Two Lairigs

Glencoe, with its rugged mountains and sweeping passes, is one of the most scenic spots in Britain and its peaks attract thousands of walkers and climbers each year. This route does not rise to the heights of the many Munros in the area but weaves a course between two of the best known, Buachaille Etive Mor and its slightly smaller side-kick, Buachaille Etive Beag. Throughout, the walk is dominated by dramatic mountain scenery and, on a good clear day, the view down Glen Etive from Lairig Gartain can only be described as breathtaking.

A wide path rises from the main A82 as it twists through the **Pass of Glencoe**, opposite a large stone memorial cairn built by the roadside. A sign for **Glen Etive** marks the way. From here, the route climbs quite steeply at first but soon eases off as you leave the noise of traffic behind. Continue until the path crosses the **Allt Lairig Eilde**. As the way rises into the glen it crosses the burn again, then a line of low cairns guides you to the col. Ahead the steep craggy north face of Stob Coire Sgreamhach dominates the view and there are a couple of spectacularly narrow waterfalls cascading down its slopes.

At the col, views into Glen Etive open out. To the south, the craggy summit of Ben Starav can be seen standing above Loch Etive. Once over the top, the route drops quickly, following the burn down the glen. Descend for a mile towards

Dalness and you will reach a junction with a path dropping left to cross the burn below a small waterfall. Cross the stream and a narrow path cuts through the grass, skirting round the lower slope of Stob Dubh then climbs quite steeply into **Lairig Gartain**. The route follows the Allt Gartain closely. Here too are great views down Glen Etive. Pause briefly as you ascend to catch your breath and take in the stunning mountain scenery. Continue up until you reach the highest point.

As you stand at the top looking north-east, a wide, sweeping glen opens out before you, separating the large and small **Buachaille Etives** on either side. The path, initially a bit boggy and indistinct in places, follows the burn and, after a long walk down, eventually emerges on to the **A82** at a large layby. Cross the road and on the far side pick up the path in the heather. Follow this west as it runs parallel to the main road. The way here is part of the old road

through the glen.

Owned by the National Trust for Scotland since the 1930s, the glen is best known for one single event in its history – the Massacre of Glencoe. In 1692 the clan chief Alistair Macdonald failed to take an oath of allegiance to King William III. On January 16, two weeks after the deadline, the king gave orders for the destruction of the Macdonalds of Glencoe. The job was entrusted to the Campbells of Glenlyon who slaughtered 38 men, women and children.

Continue west and the path rejoins the main road close to the starting point of the walk.

9 miles/14.4km
Moderate, full day walk
Obvious path through mountain glens. This walk is suitable for well equipped, fit walkers and teenage children. In winter Glencoe, even the mountain passes, can become inhospitable due to the weather. Sheep grazing so dogs on the lead.

Maps: OS Landranger, sheet 41, Harvey's Glencoe.

Start/Parking: A82 road in Pass of Glencoe. GR: NN 187563. There are large roadside laybys at and near start.

Log on to this walk at:
www.walkscotland.com/route53

Loch Dochard

Loch Dochard lurks in the shadow of a great ridge of craggy mountains. They dominate the view as you walk up the wide, flat valley from Victoria Bridge to this hidden stretch of water.

Leave the car park by its exit on to the main road, turn left and head north along the A8005 – the shortest stretch of 'A' road in the country – to **Victoria Bridge** and, beyond it, Forest Lodge which sits at a wide junction.

Turn left and follow the track signed 'Public footpath to Loch Etive by Glen Kinglass'. This right of way runs through a stand of Scots Pine before emerging into an open glen at a gate a short distance on. Stay on the track as it curves down towards the Abhainn Shira.

The track passes a tiny green hut that once housed a small school. It is now used by Glasgow University mountaineering club and can apparently house as many as 20 people! Cross Allt Toaig on a flat wooden bridge and you arrives at a ladder stile and gate at the start of the next plantation. Don't enter the forest but fork left, following a green Scottish Rights of Way Society signpost marking the 'Public footpath to Loch Etive'. The path is narrow but reasonably solid, although there are one or two boggy patches and a couple of small streams to cross.

It meets up with a track below the farm at **Clashgour**. Cross the Allt Ghabhar at a wooden suspension bridge, turn right and take the track up to **Loch Dochard**. It's rough and there's a bit of a climb but you soon emerge at a small wooden stable above the water. The loch sits in a wide coire below a ridge of high hills, huge slabs of dark rocks protecting the steep peaks. Continue along the track a little way and a small bracken-covered promontory makes a fine picnic spot. Retrace your steps back down to the suspension bridge, admiring fine views down the glen and impressive waterfalls to the left.

Don't cross the suspension bridge but head straight on along the track towards a stand of pine trees on the east side of the Allt Suilna Curra. Don't cross the stream here, but head up the right bank a little way to a narrow wooden footbridge. Cross and then climb over a ladder stile into the forestry beyond. Walk up the fence line a short distance to a break on the left and follow this until it joins a track.

The forest road passes through two high gates and, a mile on, reaches a T-junction. Turn right and climb up over the shoulder of the hill. The track curves round to a monument standing in the ruins of a croft called **Druimliart**, just beyond a low gate. From here, it's downhill to the end. There's one further high gate to negotiate before the track emerges at the car park.

8 miles/13km
Moderate, full day walk
Good track and path through open glen to remote loch, returning on forest road. High gates on the forest road are often locked and agility is required to climb them. Suitable for fairly fit adults and older children.

Map: OS Landranger, sheet 50.

Start/Parking: Public car park near Victoria Bridge. This is reached by leaving the A85 at Bridge of Orchy Hotel and following the A8005. GR: NN 271418.

Log on to this walk at:
www.walkscotland.com/route54

Tyndrum to Bridge of Orchy

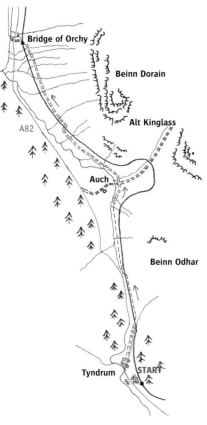

The West Highland Line is one of the most scenic railway journeys in the world. This linear walk follows the track from Tyndrum to Bridge of Orchy, in the shadow of mighty Ben Dorain. Once complete, hop on the train at Bridge of Orchy to make the return leg.

From the public car park adjacent to the village shop in **Tyndrum**, set off up the narrow surfaced road that runs by a couple of houses to reach the village hall at the top. The walk continues along a well-made track and heads steadily uphill with the main road over to the left. It flattens out after passing a large water tank and, a short way on, crosses the river and railway by solid stone bridges.

Cross the first of many stiles, turn left

and follow the path running north through the glen, alongside the railway. Ahead **Beinn Dorain**, a popular Munro, dominates the view.

The walk follows the West Highland Way, a long distance path stretching from Glasgow to Fort William. A way marker post (a thistle within a hexagon) keeps you right here, directing walkers along a stony path. It climbs steadily, then falls, passing beneath the railway via a narrow underpass.

Cross a stile, leading on to a wide track. Turn right and follow this alongside the Allt Coire Chailein, descending into Auch Gleann. As you round the slopes of **Beinn Odhar**, look up to the right to see the impressive horseshoe curve and viaduct that takes the railway across the glen and on to the lower flanks of Beinn Dorain.

The West Highland Line between Craigendoran, near Helensburgh and Fort William officially opened on August 11, 1894. The Swiss-style station buildings at Tyndrum and **Bridge of Orchy** are typical of the architecture on the railway. However, neither they nor the signal boxes are manned any longer – the whole line is controlled from a signalling centre at Banavie, near Fort William.

In the base of the glen, cross a bridge over the **Allt Kinglass** and, on the other side, turn left, go over a stile, and continue along the track. The route rises gently and, a little over a mile on, crosses the railway again, next to an old cottage now used by a mountaineering club.

The track skirts below the crags of Beinn Dorain, up to the right, and soon

7 miles/11km
Easy, full day walk
Well-graded, low level route with track and path throughout suitable for all ages and abilities. Sheep grazing in places, so dogs will need to go on the lead.

Map: OS Landranger, sheet 59.

Start/Parking: Public car park next to village shop and newsagent in Tyndrum. GR: NN 328307.

Log on to this walk at:
www.walkscotland.com/route55

Bridge of Orchy looms into view. The final stage is easy and brings you down to an underpass entering the station.

The best way back to Tyndrum is by train, although there are also regular bus services. If you do return by train, you will need to find your way from Tyndrum Upper station back to the car park by the shop. To do this, head down the access road from the station to join the A85. Turn right and walk north along the pavement through Tyndrum to the car park.

If you decide to make the return journey by bus, you'll find the stop on the A85 outside the Bridge of Orchy Hotel, a short walk from the station.

Pap of Glencoe

The Pap of Glencoe is perhaps one of the best-known mountain landmarks in this part of Scotland. Rising from the shores of Loch Leven the peak – Sgorr na Ciche is its Gaelic name – stands guard over the road leading into Glencoe and offers some spectacular views south to the hulk of Bidean nam Bian and west across the Ballachulish bridge and Loch Linnhe to Ardgour. As you rise into the col between the Pap and its bulky neighbour Sgorr nam Fiannaidh – a Munro at the western end of the fearsome Aonach Eagach – there are stunning vistas north-east to the Mamores, above Kinlochleven.

The ascent is relatively straightforward but hard work all the same, given you are embarking upon the 742 metre climb from just about sea level. You can either set off on foot from **Glencoe village** – about a mile west of the end of the track where you leave the surfaced road behind – or park in one of a number of small laybys (just avoid leaving your car in a passing place or at the start of the track where there are prominent 'no parking' signs).

The way leaves the road next to the edge of the forest, passing through a metal kissing gate by fenced animal enclosures. A few yards on there's an unlocked wooden gate to negotiate before the gravel track begins the ascent, rising past a cottage on the left towards a small water supply compound.

Before this is reached, an obvious path bears right, running level across the open hillside where shaggy Highland cows are often grazing. The route crosses a burn running down through a deep cutting and curves left, ascending more strenuously once again up the edge of the gorge. This is a fine test of stamina as there is little respite from the climb, other than to stop periodically to admire the view.

The gradient eases higher up as the black peaty path skirts out along the hillside towards the rocky slopes below Sgorr nam Fiannaidh, before switching back on itself to curve north into the col below the **Pap**. From here, drop down to cross a small burn and, on the other side, the climb on to the rocky summit begins. A large cairn marks the top.

Nearby there is a smaller cairn, embedded into which is an unusual memorial plaque to a two-year-old child.

Descend from the top by the route of ascent and return to the col. From here, you can return home by the same path. Alternatively, another path follows the northern side of the burn down over the open hillside. Lower down it skirts out in a north-west direction across the slope before dropping down past the water supply compound to rejoin the path next to the gravel track. Retrace your steps from here to the start.

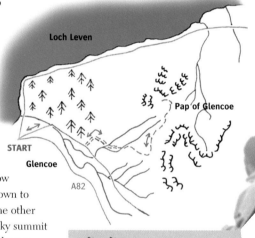

4 miles/6km

Moderate, half day walk

A steep ascent with some easy scrambling towards the summit. This walk is suitable for fairly fit adults and older children.

Maps: OS Landranger, sheet 41, Harvey's Glencoe.

Start/Parking: Glencoe village or track-end by the edge of the forest. GR NN 112586. Public car park in Glencoe village (with toilets) or small roadside laybys near track-end.

Log on to this walk at: www.walkscotland.com/route56

Loch Ossian

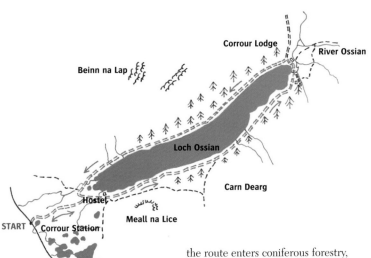

8 miles/13km
Moderate, full day walk
An easy, low-level walk on good tracks
suitable for well equipped walkers and
older children. This is, however, a
remote location where, on a bad day,
the weather can be inhospitable.

Maps: OS Landranger, sheets 41, 42.
Start/Parking: Corrour Station on the
Glasgow to Fort William West Highland
Railway. GR: NN 355664. The nearest
access by car is Rannoch Station, the next
station down from Corrour. Be careful
that you don't miss your train!

Log on to this walk at:
www.walkscotland.com/route57

These days it's hard to find true
wilderness, that is, until you travel to
lonely Corrour Station on Rannoch
Moor and wander around Loch Ossian.
Only a handful of people live on the
Corrour Estate and as there are no
roads in or out, you won't see any cars
here, except for the odd Land Rover.
Loch Ossian sits in the shadow of three
Munros. There's a shooting lodge and
estate buildings at one end and, at the
other, a basic youth hostel where tame
stags frequently gather to be fed by
the warden and his guests.

Step off the train at **Corrour Station**, the
highest station on the British rail
network, cross the line and follow the
track east across open moor. It runs
fairly level, through a landscape of
heather and boggy pools, before
dropping to the lochside hostel. The
wooden building, once a boathouse and
stable, sits among trees on a low
promontory.

At a **junction** a track on the left leads
into the **hostel** and a path on the right is
signed for Rannoch. Avoid these and
carry straight on along the lochside,
passing by a couple of small tree-cove
islands just offshore. Two kilometres o

the route enters coniferous forestry,
initially sparsely planted but then more
dense. The track remains close to the
water and there are strips of pleasant
sandy beach that make ideal rest spots.

Continue until you reach the far end
of the loch, not long after a high gate
and stile. The track curves left past an
estate house, then crosses the **River
Ossian**. On the far side there's a white
gate and a grey stone wall. Don't go
through the gate but follow the track as
it skirts to the right, round the wall. It
passes **Corrour Lodge** before reaching a
junction where a memorial to former
estate owner Sir John Stirling Maxwell
stands. The right-hand road runs off
through Strath Ossian. Our route,
however, goes left along the north shore
of the loch, passing a couple of high
gates by way of ladder stiles. There are

excellent views over the water to **Carn
Dearg**, a Munro. Keep an eye out for the
occasional tree-lined peninsula offering a
good viewpoint down the loch.

Three miles from the lodge the track
leaves the forest and runs over open
moorland, curving round the west end of
the loch. This is the most scenic stretch
of water, dotted with small islands heavy
with pine trees. The way meets up with
the main track just above the youth
hostel. From here, retrace your steps
back to Corrour Station.

Ben Lawers

Ben Lawers – Britain's tenth highest peak – dominates the picture postcard scene of Loch Tay when viewed from Kenmore and, on a clear day, provides an awesome perch from which most of Scotland can be seen unfolding around you.

This particular hill benefits – or rather suffers (depending on your point of view) – from a **visitor centre** built on the unclassified road between the **A827** Loch Tay road and Glen Lyon to the north. Because of its blissful situation high above the gently curving loch, this is always going to be a popular destination for walkers and the centre simply adds to this.

Ben Lawers is, therefore, never a place for those looking for solitude, except in all but the most testing conditions. On the other hand, the small revenue generated by the centre is put to good use by conservationists who are at least attempting to make sure that there isn't too much tourist erosion.

This walk follows the wishes of the landowner, the National Trust for Scotland, and tackles the 1214-metre high peak via its 1103-metre high neighbour, **Beinn Ghlas**. Leaving your transport in the ample car park at the centre, follow the wooden walkway that splits in two with one branch signposted as a nature trail and the other indicating the path for Ben Lawers.

Glance over your left shoulder at this point to Meall nan Tarmachan which is a wonderfully rough and rocky alternative to the grassy plains of Beinn Ghlas ahead. The obvious path follows the line of the burn, passing some ruined shielings, and continues up the steep slope before zig-zagging.

The way flattens out before the final stiff pull to the summit of Beinn Ghlas, which provides a tantalising view of the day's destination.

Head down from the summit into the col between Beinn Ghlas and its illustrious neighbour. Your legs and lungs will enjoy the break before tackling the imposing eastern face of Ben Lawers.

Work to combat erosion on the broken granite upper reaches of the mountain is obvious as you make the slog through the schist to the top with its trig point and stone cairn.

Hikers who have managed to leave a car in the tiny hamlet of Lawers can continue their adventure by following the ridge to Creag an Fhithic and then bagging An Stuic (recently elevated to Munro status) before continuing over Meall Garbh and Meall Greigh to complete a worthy five-Munro expedition.

To finish this walk, however, retrace your steps over Beinn Ghlas to the visitor centre.

5 miles/8km
Challenging, full day walk
A tough ascent suitable for fit, experienced hillwalkers and teenage children. The summit of Ben Lawers should never be underestimated even on an apparently good day. Full weather and navigational equipment must be carried at all times. In winter conditions can be bad and when the mountains are under snow, this route's only for experienced hillwalkers with crampons and ice-axes, and the knowledge to use them.

Maps: OS Landranger, sheet 51, Harvey's Ben Lawers.

Start/Parking: Ben Lawers visitor centre, near Killin. GR: NN 609380.

Log on to this walk at:
www.walkscotland.com/route58

Stuchd an Lochain

Tucked away towards the top of the 'the longest, loneliest and loveliest glen in Scotland', Stuchd an Lochain is one of the best vantage points from which to savour the scenic delights of Glen Lyon. But that's not all. From the top on a clear day you'll also see Rannoch Moor and the mountains of Glencoe.

Start below the **Giorra Dam**, where the road ends. Cross the bridge over the outflow (a locked five-bar gate must be negotiated) and head up the track as it loops quite steeply up through small plantations to the south end of the dam. The huge wall of concrete holds back **Loch an Daimh**, a reservoir created for generating electricity.

The track skirts round the southern shore of the loch and a short way on look out for a small cairn on the left which

6 miles/10km

Challenging, full day walk

A straightforward Munro for experienced hillwalkers and teenage children. Dogs will have to go on lead throughout due to sheep grazing. In winter it is a more serious proposition and when the mountains are under snow, this is a route for experienced hillwalkers with crampons and ice-axes and the knowledge to use them. Deer stalking takes place on this estate from August through to February and during this time walkers should stick to established paths and ridges – as this route does. There is no stalking on Sundays.

Map: OS Landranger, sheet 51.

Start/Parking: Giorra Dam at the head of Loch an Daimh. GR: NN 510464.

Log on to this walk at:
www.walkscotland.com/route59

marks the start of the **Stuchd an Lochain** path. This rises along the hillside for a way, crossing a handful of tiny burns, before curving left to climb more steeply through grass and heather, following a bubbling burn upstream. It is wet and muddy underfoot and remains so until you reach an outcrop of brilliant white quartz much higher up.

Not long after this the path rises on to a broad shoulder where it meets a line of rusty fence posts. Turn right at this point and follow the posts west on to the stony summit of Creag an Fheadain. This is the first point on the route with a view of the summit of Stuchd an Lochain and it's an impressive sight.

She's a shy mountain, in that she seems to hide her true grace until almost the very last minute. Approaching from Glen Lyon, the hill appears to be an unremarkable lump of rock and vegetation. However, as you get closer, you discover there's much more to Stuchd an Lochain.

Viewed from Creag an Fheadain, the top is an almost perfect triangle, the steep grassy eastern face strewn with rocky crags. Nestling in the dark coire

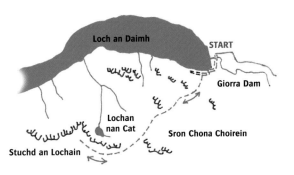

below is **Lochan nan Cat** and the name Stuchd an Lochain translates from Gaelic as peak of the little loch.

The top of this outlier is a fine spot for views east down Glen Lyon and to the Lawers ridge, eight miles distant as the crow flies.

The fence posts remain your guide as they lead south down into the col and then up on to **Sron Chona Choirein**. You may spot herds of red deer lurking in the coires on either side. The path curves right as you ascend and the gradient eases off significantly to offer a fairly level walk west towards Stuchd an Lochain. A final short but strenuous pull brings you up on to the summit where there's a cairn.

To finish the walk, retrace your steps back down to the dam.

Ben Chonzie

Rising between Strathearn and Loch Tay, Ben Chonzie – sometimes referred to as Ben-y-Hone – is a solitary Munro but one well worth seeking out. The route to the top is fairly straightforward and takes you through some very pleasant open country with fine views over Perthshire and the Southern Highlands.

9 miles/14.5km
Challenging, full day walk
A route for reasonably experienced and fit hillwalkers and older children. Dogs should be on the lead due to sheep grazing and ground nesting birds in a conservation area. In winter it is a more serious proposition and when the mountains are under snow, this is a route for experienced hillwalkers with crampons and ice-axes and the knowledge of how to use them.

Map: OS Landranger, sheet 52.

Start/Parking: Coishavachan in Glen Lednock, four miles north of Comrie. GR: NN 743273. There is a small parking area at the start. This can be reached by following the single track Glen Lednock road from Comrie. Please don't obstruct the access track to Coishavachan.

Log on to this walk at:
www.walkscotland.com/route60

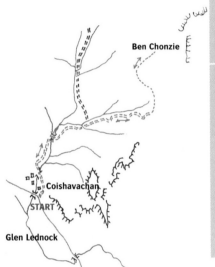

From the car park, follow a track north, signed for Ardtalnaig. This skirts between open fields to reach a cluster of cottages at **Coishavachan** a short distance on. Bear right at a public footpath sign and follow the track along the front of the buildings to a gate. Go through and the way curves left to lead out over open country, passing patches of woodland and a small pond on the left.

It rises very gradually, twisting left to cross the Invergeldie Burn and passes through another gate. From here, the track begins to rise, curving right to follow the stream uphill. As you ascend, **Ben Chonzie** (931 metres) looms into view over on the right. Further up there's another gate to go through as you enter a conservation area where efforts are being made to protect ground-nesting birds.

Ignore a grassy track on the left a short way on and follow the main route as its drops to the right to cross a dry burn, the water drained from it by a concrete dam above. On the other side, the track curves right over the open hillside, before cutting back to climb through the heather.

About a kilometre on from the dam, you will arrive at a junction of tracks. The route on your left crosses a small burn and leads through the glen to eventually reach Ardtalnaig, on the south shore of Loch Tay. Don't take this but carry straight on up, following the track over the hillside until you reach a cairn about a mile on where a path branches off on the left. Take this.

The way is a little indistinct in places and can be wet underfoot. As long as you continue to go up you can't go far wrong. It rises on to a broad shoulder, dissected by a line of rusty old fence posts. When you reach these, bear left and follow them north-west along the broad ridge. As you go, keep an eye out for mountain hare – Ben Chonzie (pronounced 'ben ee hoan') has a healthy population of these creatures. The fence line makes a sharp right turn. Continue to follow it over increasingly stony ground and it will lead you to the top. A large stone enclosure where you can shelter from the elements marks the summit. Here you can enjoy views south over Loch Turret to Crieff. To the north, on a clear day, the Ben Lawers range is visible.

To return to the start, retrace your steps to Coishavachan.

Pitlochry to Killiecrankie

Killiecrankie is perhaps best known for its 'soldier's leap', the spot where a fleeing government trooper flung himself across the river gorge to evade capture by the victorious Jacobite fighters following the Battle of Killiecrankie in 1689. This route visits that famous spot, but thankfully there is no need for walkers to follow his example!

The best starting point for this walk is the tourist information centre in the heart of **Pitlochry**. From there, head west along Atholl Road, passing through Pitlochry's main shopping thoroughfare. Continue to the far end and turn right up Larchwood Road.

A mile on from the junction, the road turns sharp left and, a short way on, reaches a junction on the edge of the hamlet of **Moulin**. Follow the road north to reach a small car park and continue ahead on a path heading up through the trees, past a small burn down to the right. The way rises steadily to meet a track and, on the other side, continues straight ahead, this time with the stream cutting a channel through the rocks to the left. Rising more steeply, the way climbs to meet a fence bordering an open field and track and follows it for a short distance with Ben Vrackie in view up ahead. Join the track a short distance on and follow for a hundred metres or so until the path picks up again on the right.

It crosses the burn by a wooden footbridge and heads north through mixed woodland before reaching a ladder stile at the top of the woods. With the confines of the conifers now behind, an obvious path rises over open moorland, passing beneath a line of overhead cables. As you gain height, views open out over Pitlochry and the Tummel valley to the south. Sheep graze the hillside here but you may also be lucky enough to see grouse, roe deer and mountain hare. The path climbs steadily to reach a junction where the route up to the bealach branches off on the left. Take this and an energetic climb rises into the col below **Meall na Aodainn Moire**. This is known as the Bealach na

Searmoin, pass of the sermon.

Once over, the path descends over open moorland to join a track lower down. Stay on this as it curves down through a series of hairpin bends towards Old Faskally Farm where it curves left to head for **Killiecrankie**, passing below the A9. It drops to meet the B8079 a very short distance on. Cross the road to reach the National Trust for Scotland's Killiecrankie visitor centre.

From here the walk heads south through the Pass of Killiecrankie, following the River Garry south and sticking quite closely to the east bank.

The route passes under **Garry Bridge** and stays with the river all the way to **Loch Faskally**. The path passes below the A9 again before joining a track, which leads up into Pitlochry and on to Atholl Road. Follow this back to the tourist centre.

10 miles/17km
Moderate, full day walk
A long walk over open moor and through forestry with tracks and paths throughout. Suitable for fit walkers and older children.

Maps: OS Landranger, sheet 43 and 52.

Start/Parking: Pitlochry Tourist Information Centre, Atholl Road. GR: NN 941581. Public car park next to tourist information centre.

Log on to this walk at:
www.walkscotland.com/route61

Pitmedden Forest

When you enter Pitmedden Forest it's as if you're taking a step back in time. Let your imagination run riot as you wander through the trees. Visualise the kings and queens of Scotland tracking wild boar, the clatter of hooves and the yapping of dogs. For the woodland sits within the hunting ground of Falkland Palace, a favourite haunt of Mary, Queen of Scots. To encourage recreational use, a small car park has been provided, along with various waymarked routes for cyclists and walkers.

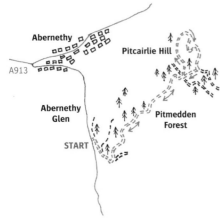

From the car park, the track rises south, running parallel with the public road through **Abernethy Glen** for a short distance before it curves left to reach a junction. Ignore the route on the left and continue along the main track, which goes on climbing, curving left to reach another junction a short way on. Go left here, the track rising gently through tall stands of predominantly Scots Pine trees, curving right and then left. During the First World War **Pitmedden Forest** was a much-needed source of wood. It was later replanted with Scots Pine, Sitka and Norway Spruce by the Forestry Commission and continues to be used as a commercial plantation.

There's a clearing a short way on and another junction where a grassy track strikes off on the left. However, stay with the main track as it heads back into the trees, descending slightly before it starts to rise once again.

Further on, the route twists and turns a couple of times to reach the edge of the forest where views open out south to the Lomond Hills, the prominent rounded summits of East Lomond and West Lomond easily recognisable.

The track skirts the edge of the plantation, bordering land invaded by spiky gorse bushes. Fields slope into the valley below and views stretch out across the fertile Howe of Fife. The way curves past an open area of ground, descending to another junction. Ignore the track on the left, which leads to the farm at Stewartshill, and carry straight on, round a barrier gate, to a crossroads. Turn left here and the track leads north, lined with wild raspberry plants and blaeberry bushes that provide a refreshing snack for walkers towards the end of July and during early August when the fruit is ripe for the picking.

Curving right, the way climbs under electricity pylon lines before turning east and then south, heading back under the wires. It rises around the northern flank of **Pitcairlie Hill**, passing below the line twice more. It then heads south to reach a junction. Turn right here and descend to the crossroads met earlier in the walk. From here, retrace your steps back down the forest track to the car park.

7.5 miles/12km
Moderate, half day walk
Easy to follow forest tracks throughout. Suitable for all ages and abilities. Keep an eye out for mountain bikes and occasional vehicles using the tracks. This route is suitable for mountain bikes throughout.

Map: OS Landranger, sheet 58.

Start/Parking: Pitmedden Forest car park, Abernethy Glen. GR: NO 188141.

Log on to this walk at:
www.walkscotland.com/route62

Deuchny Woods and Binn Hill

Deuchny Woods and Binn Hill, near Perth, have long been popular with local walkers, whether out for a Sunday afternoon leg stretch or giving the dog its daily exercise. By combining the pair, you can enjoy a pleasant woodland walk with a detour to an old stone tower standing watch over the fertile lands of the Carse of Gowrie.

3 miles/4.8km
Easy, half day walk
An easy woodland walk with track and path throughout. Suitable for all ages and abilities.

Map: OS Landranger, sheet 58.

Start/Parking: Forestry Commission Jubilee car park. GR: NO 145236. To reach this follow the road out of Perth from Perth Bridge, up past Murray Royal Hospital and continue out into the countryside for a mile and a half.

Log on to this walk at:
www.walkscotland.com/route63

straight on and the Coronation Road emerges into the open at a gate on the edge of the woodland.

A path drops to the right to cross a grassy field and the way sticks with the fence as it runs south, negotiating a marshy spot using makeshift stepping stones. Beyond a gate, the path rises to the steading at **Northlees**. The path is signed through the farmyard and joins a track leading down to the public road.

Once on the road, turn right and follow it up to the bottom corner of **Deuchny Woods**. When you reach this point, turn left on a track leading to a small unofficial car park at **Binn Hill**. A track on the right passes through a gate and heads west along the side of the hill. At its end, a small path on the left climbs through the trees to Binn Tower, a folly built in the early part of the 19th century. From here you can look over the River Tay to Fife.

Continue along the path as it curves round, returning to the unofficial parking area. Walk back to the road, turn left and, on the other side a few yards on, a narrow path climbs into the trees and over a recently felled portion to join a wide track.

Turn left and the forest road takes you round the hillside, with views to neighbouring **Kinnoull Hill** with its equally impressive cliff-top tower. At the next junction, go left and the track leads you back to the start of the walk.

Leave the Jubilee car park at its northern end, turn right and follow a steep track up to a gate and water tower. Turn left here and the way flattens out to contour round the hillside, passing through woodland of tall pine trees. It curves right and, a short way after the bend, a path branches left. Follow this down to cross a fence and join the Coronation Road, an ancient right of way. Turn right and the track, often used by pony trekkers, leaves the woodland and heads out over an open field, bearing right to meet the Langley Burn. Underfoot, the way can be quite wet and muddy here as you follow the burn upstream through a sheltered valley.

A gate leads back into the Forestry Commission plantation and, carrying straight on through the base of the glen, in a wide break in the trees there's a good track which makes for easy walking and you'll soon reach a T-junction. Carry

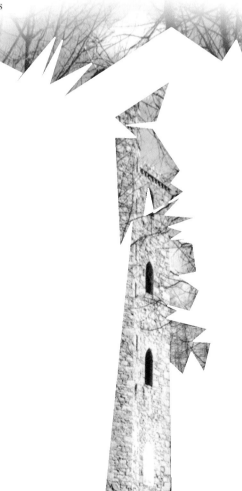

Falls of Acharn

Perthshire's countryside is full of history. Many of the best examples are to be found around Loch Tay, and on this walk some obvious remains can be seen. One example is the small but well preserved stone circle occupying an airy roost on the open hillside overlooking the loch. Above the Falls of Acharn is a hermit's cave. Even though evidence suggests this is a much more recent, tourist-oriented addition to the landscape, it is well worth exploring and the underground passageway will doubtless keep children amused.

From the east side of the road bridge in **Acharn**, head south up a minor road, past Old Mill Cottage and a red telephone box. The path rises quite steeply to a wooden fence. Bear right of this and climb to a wooden bridge above small waterfalls. Don't cross but continue up the left side of the burn, with the path hemmed in between two fences, to a kissing gate at the top. Go through the gate to join a track by a stone bridge over the burn. Turn left. Go through a wooden gate and follow the main track as it curves right and then left to run east over open hillside.

The route reaches a junction above the **Remony Burn**. Bear right and follow the track up over an open grassy field.

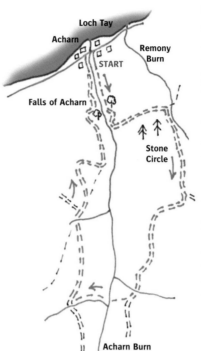

The way is a little indistinct but soon becomes much more obvious as you approach a gate. Go through – up to the right is a stone circle with excellent views to the Ben Lawers range and Schiehallion.

Back on the track, continue over open moorland to a junction. Turn right here and follow the track into a small

plantation of Scots Pines, with views over **Loch Tay**. The track curves south again and, after a brief climb, descends over open hillside. At its lowest point, just beyond a burn crossing, a smaller track branches off to the right. Follow this down to cross the **Acharn Burn**. There's no bridge, but just upstream from where the track fords the water there is a line of stones that act as a good crossing point.

Once safely over, follow the steep track up to a small wooden shed on the hillside above. Turn right at the hut and take the track north, descending over open hillside. At the next junction, bear right and continue on the main track down to grazing fields above Acharn. The route emerges at a gate above the **Falls of Acharn**.

Beyond this, turn left and descend to the Hermit's Cave on the right. This is well worth exploring, as the short, dimly-lit underground passage leads to a viewpoint opposite the Falls of Acharn. The tunnel comes out again further down the track. Continue to Acharn and join the road opposite a horn carver's workshop. Turn right to return to the start.

6 miles/10km
Easy, half day walk
Path up through woodland and tracks over open hillside and moor. There is some fairly easy ascent. Suitable for all ages and abilities

Maps: OS Landranger, sheet 51.

Start/Parking: Bridge over the Acharn Burn in Acharn, a mile and a half west of Kenmore on the south Loch Tay road. GR: NN 756438. Leave cars to the east of the bridge on the roadside.

Log on to this walk at:
www.walkscotland.com/route64

Ben Vrackie

Standing proud at 841 metres high, Ben Vrackie has all the presence of a much taller peak. It falls short of Munro status by a touch over 80 metres, but the hike to the summit of this uniquely individual Perthshire Corbett is every bit as challenging and satisfying as an ascent of a far loftier peak

The path to the top of **Ben Vrackie** climbs through a landscape with much contrast, blending all the best ingredients of the Scottish countryside. It begins in peaceful woodland, strikes out over untamed moor, strokes the shoreline of a tranquil little lochan and, for the grand finale, twists up through unyielding boulders to peak on the summit.

From the car park above **Moulin**, set off up the path which heads north through the trees, accompanied by a small burn down to the right. It climbs gently to a track. Cross over and, on the other side, continue straight ahead, this time with the stream on the left.

The way rises to a fence bordering an open field and track. Path and track run parallel for a short distance with the mountain in view ahead. The track is soon joined and followed for a hundred metres or so until the path is picked up again on the right.

The way crosses the burn at a wooden footbridge and continues north through mixed woodland before rising through a leafy ride in the dense plantation of larch to a ladder stile at the top.

Striking out over open heather moor from here, the path passes under a line of overhead cables and climbs steadily to a well placed bench, an ideal chance to catch your breath and admire the views south over the River Tummel, in the valley below.

Not far beyond the seat is a ladder stile and, after this, the way flattens out before descending to **Loch a'Choire**, a peaceful stretch of water sheltered by the rock and scree-strewn bulk of Ben Vrackie. It is this stony facade and the effect of glittering sunlight upon the rocks that gives the hill its name – Ben Vrackie translates from the Gaelic as 'speckled mountain'.

By following the path to the east end of the lochan and then over the embankment at its head you avoid a marshy patch of ground. From the far end of this mound, the ascent proper begins. The path negotiates a low ridge, then climbs steadily, and steeply, into a shallow coire to the east of the top, lurking enticingly above a fortress-like barrage of jutting crags.

Although it may look impossible to breach such defences, there is a way. Stay with the path as it curves left for the final pull through rocks to the top. It boasts a trig point and a cairn complete with panoramic viewfinder highlighting various features of interest in the surrounding landscape.

Neighbouring Carn Liath and Beinn a'Ghlo fill the view to the north while, to the south, Strath Tay stretches far off into the distance.

To return to Moulin, retrace your steps.

5 miles/8km
Moderate, half day walk
A strenuous ascent best tackled by fit walkers and older children. The final stretch from Loch a'Choire is steep and the summit exposed.

Map: OS Landranger, sheet 43 and 52.

Start/Parking: Small car park, signed on the road from Moulin. Turn left immediately behind the hotel in the centre of the village. The car park is small and can be busy, particularly at weekends. GR: NN 944596.

Log on to this walk at:
www.walkscotland.com/route65

Deuchary Hill

At just over 500 metres in height, Deuchary Hill is a relatively small peak compared to some of Scotland's more majestic mountains, but its hefty flanks are high enough to offer the walker an unbeatable viewpoint over the surrounding countryside.

Leave the car park by its main entrance and head down the track for a short distance. Turn left and enter Atholl Estate. Stay with the main route heading north, passing by **Cally Loch** on the right. Although masked by trees you should be able to snatch a glimpse of this picturesque stretch of water. The track continues north, passing isolated houses at **Hatton** and Birkenburn until it reaches a high gate at **The Glack**, a remote pair of cottages. Go through the gate and the way curves up to reach the southern end of **Mill Dam**. Just before you reach the water, a path branches off to the right, entering trees skirting the edge of the water and this soon begins to climb over bracken-covered hillside.

Towards the top of the incline, you cross a lively little burn by an old stone bridge. Immediately after this, a path

branches off to the right. Don't take this but carry straight on. The track climbs through a cleft between **Deuchary Hill** and a small outlying knoll and continues to ascend before finally flattening off. In due course, the route curves right and a track cuts across your path. Turn right here and follow it up to **Lochan na Beinne**. From there it's a fairly short pull over open hillside to the summit of Deuchary Hill. Enjoy the panoramic views then return to the lochan and follow the track back down to the junction. Turn right here and head along the track to **Loch Ordie**, the way descending towards the water by **Lochordie Lodge**, a row of cottages.

Go left at the cottages, following a track through rhododendron bushes to a bridge over Loch Ordie's outflow. Beyond this, go left and follow this substantial track down to Raor Lodge. When you reach the farm steading,

turn right down the next track passing through a gate and then a stretch of tall mixed woodland. After a kilometre of descent, the track reaches a gate and, beyond this, meets another track. Turn left and follow this as it rises steadily through farmland and above Rotmell Farm. The way continues to gain height gently above the **A9** and River Tay in the base of the wide Strathtay valley.

At the end of the fields, the route enters Atholl Forest. Carry straight on, ignoring a track on the left, to reach a high gate at the edge of a plantation of larch. The track runs level for a way before descending to a minor road. Turn left and follow the road east for about half a kilometre along a wide grassy verge until you reach **Polnie Loch**. A path on the left runs along the shore of the loch and leads up through trees to the car park.

12 miles/19km
Challenging, full day walk
A long walk with track and path through forestry and over open moor. Suitable for fit adults and older children. Sections of the route run through grazing land where dogs will need to go on the lead.

Map: OS Landranger, sheet 52 or 53.

Start/Parking: Caley car park, Dunkeld. GR: NN 023437. To reach this, follow the A923 north through Dunkeld and turn right at a junction signed for Blairgowrie. The car park access track is second on the left (there's a post box at the junction).

Log on to this walk at:
www.walkscotland.com/route66

Two Distilleries Tour

Whisky is produced in more or less the same way across Scotland. However, the distilleries from which the nation's favourite tipple spills all have their own unique characters. Nowhere is this more obvious than in the Perthshire town of Pitlochry, home to the country's smallest distillery, Edradour, and one of its most productive, Blair Athol. This walk links the pair, giving you ample opportunity to sample a dram or two (parents only, of course!).

of its most attractive ditilleries, with a gurgling burn, trim lawns and colourful beds of flowers.

Malt whisky has been distilled here since 1825 and it is one of the last in Scotland to produce a handcrafted malt in limited quantities, turning out around a dozen casks a week. There's a guided tour on which visitors can view traditional whisky making techniques. Edradour is open seven days a week from March to the end of October and from Monday to Saturday from November to mid-December.

From the distillery, follow the road north as it climbs and curves out of Milton of Edradour. The way flattens off, running through open fields with views over Pitlochry and the broad Tummel valley below. When you reach a sign for **Pitlochry** in the hedgerow, leave the road and take a path on the left. This descends past **Edradour House** and Edradour School.

When it joins a track, turn left, following another sign for Pitlochry, and continue down to Black Spout Wood, entering the trees beyond a gate. Follow yellow waymarkers through the woodland and cross the Kinnaird Burn at a footbridge. Turn left on the other side and the main path runs parallel with the stream to a single track road

Go left and follow the road down to the **A924** where the route bears left again, passing below the railway and by the Holy Trinity Church. Continue along the pavement to reach **Blair Athol Distillery**.

From the **Black Spout Wood** car park, follow a yellow waymarker for the **Edradour** walk. A good track runs along the edge of a golf course before curving right at a junction, climbing to a viewing platform overlooking the impressive **Black Spout** waterfall.

The way continues to rise through oak woodland, staying close to the Edradour Burn. Follow yellow waymarkers and signs for Edradour and the path emerges into the open, continuing between trees on the right and open fields to the left, offering a fine view to Ben Vrackie.

After passing a cottage, the way arrives in **Milton of Edradour**. The cluster of neat white buildings with bright red doors beyond a car park is the first of the day's distilleries. Edradour is not only Scotland's smallest, but also one

3 miles/5km
Easy, half day walk
Easy walk through woodland and farmland with good paths throughout, although these can be muddy in places. Suitable for all.

Map: OS Landranger, sheet 52.

Start/Parking: Black Spout Wood car park, Pitlochry. GR: NN 952574.

Log on to this walk at:
www.walkscotland.com/route67

While the basic whisky-making process employed here is the same as at Edradour, everything is done on a much larger scale. Drawing its water from the Allt Dour burn, Blair Athol produces the eight-year-old Bell's Extra Special. It is open seven days from Easter to September and Monday to Friday from October to Easter with restricted opening hours during the rest of the year.

From here, follow the pavement of the main road east back at the Black Spout Wood car park.

Clunie Wood

Pitlochry has long been a popular spot with visitors and as many of us like nothing better than a good walk, landowners and the local authority have banded together to create a series of marked trails. The walk through Clunie Wood is one such route.

On the west side of the larger of the two Ferry Road car parks there is a walk information board and, next to it, an exit. Go through, turn left and a track leads towards a cottage. Bear left before the cottage and the way rises past a shed into the trees. It skirts caravans and drops to a road opposite a bungalow. Cross and follow a tarmac path between

houses and a small stream and parkland to reach a suspension bridge over the River Tummel.

Cross to **Port-na-Craig** where the path joins a road. Turn left and follow this up to its next junction. A minor road rises on the other side to reach the A9. Cross over and on the other side a single-track road leads to **Middleton of Fonab** farm. Go straight on past a cottage further up to a gate and the track rises under a line of pylons to enter woodland.

In the trees, the way curves right to a gate. Don't go through this, but stay with the track as it swings left. Beyond the next right-hand bend, a path branches off to the left, signed for Clunie Walk. Pass through a kissing gate and a grassy path rises through the forest. It climbs for about a kilometre to cross a track and continues up, levelling off to reach a crossroads.

Turn right and walk north-west to a high gate at the edge of the forest. The track curves steeply to the right, rising to a **mast** on

7 miles/11km
Moderate, half day walk
Track and path through forest with a moderately steep ascent early on. Care must be taken crossing the busy A9 trunk road in the early and latter stages of the route.

Map: OS Landranger, sheet 52.

Start/Parking: Ferry Road car park, Pitlochry. GR: NN 938580. A parking charge is levied.

Log on to this walk at:
www.walkscotland.com/route68

An Suidhe. From the gate, a path heads out over open heather moorland. It can be indistinct in places but there are a handful of waymarkers to keep you on course. It runs north-west for a distance before curving north east, following an old Pictish road down to **Clunie Wood**.

Cross a metal ladder stile and follow the path to a junction. Turn right and head through the woodland to a clearing with pylons. Turn right here at a waymarker and follow the track to the next junction a short way on. Continue straight on, following the pylons up the hill. The track curves right into the trees, swinging out to the edge of the plantation, then left back to the clearing. It passes under the wires before curving down under the line again and across a wide clearing. Follow the track on to the next junction.

At another clearing there is a junction. Turn right up through a gate and the track climbs gently, joining a more substantial forest road a short way on. At a Y-shaped junction, turn left and the track curves down to a metal gate, with views over Pitlochry to Ben Vrackie to enjoy as you descend. Go through the gate and you'll reach the track used earlier. Retrace steps to the start from here.

Drummond Hill

Drummond Hill at the north-east end of Loch Tay is criss-crossed by forestry tracks and paths which combine to provide a network of routes for walkers and mountain bikers. This outing climbs to the northern summit, home to a tall aerial standing proud above the surrounding trees, and takes in a viewpoint where there are panoramas over Loch Tay and Kenmore, a picturesque village at the head of the loch.

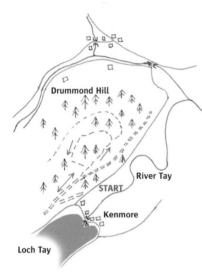

The route encompasses both wide tracks and more discreet pathways where rusty red carpets of pine needle wind their way through the trees, sunlight penetrating the canopy of branches above to spray bright shafts of sunlight on to the forest floor. Try this walk first then explore the many other highways and byways of **Drummond Hill**.

Pass through a kissing gate at the top end of the car park and follow a wide forestry track lined with silver birch trees, tall pines and rhododendron bushes. The track passes a metal tank on the right to reach a junction where there is a wooden sign pointing to a 'viewpoint'. Turn right here and follow the track as it rises through the birch, beech and larch trees lining the bracken-covered hillside. Occasional glimpses of **Kenmore** and **Loch Tay** can be snatched through breaks in the woodland cover. The track curves left, passing a small mesh enclosure, to arrive at a wide junction. Cross the track running from right to left and continue up a track on the opposite side. This disappears into dense coniferous forestry.

A kilometre on, the track reaches a fork where there is a black mountain bike route marker post. Take the left and prepare for a strenuous climb to the top of the hill. The way is open but thick woodland lines the route and there are plastic reflector posts placed at intervals. The track curves left and after a stiff pull emerges at a tall metal aerial sited within a fenced compound of sheds. A narrow path branches right just before this to a viewpoint on top of an open mound.

As the track approaches the gate to the compound, it passes through a stone wall. Before it does, a path bears off to the right, following the wall into the forest. Take this and descend through tall Scots Pine trees. Stay with the wall and avoid a couple of sets of tracks on the right. The path levels out at a T-junction where there are mountain bike marker posts again. Go left here and descend across an open area of bracken and larch to enter the trees again.

When you emerge on to a track at the bottom of the path, turn right to reach the wide junction again. Head west along the track to the wooded viewpoint a kilometre on. This makes an ideal picnic spot. From there, r... steps to the start.

5 miles/8km
Moderate, half day walk
Forestry track and path with some ascent. Suitable for fairly fit adults and older children.

Map: OS Landranger, sheet 51 or 52.

Start/Parking: Mains of Taymouth Forestry Commission car park. GR: NN 772460.

Log on to this walk at:
www.walkscotland.com/route69

Birks of Aberfeldy

The poet Robbie Burns fell in love with the Birks of Aberfeldy when he visited in 1787. So enchanted was he by the spectacular waterfalls and the lush greenery of the Den of Moness, that he wrote a song, to share his discovery with those who had not been so fortunate as to see the spot for themselves.

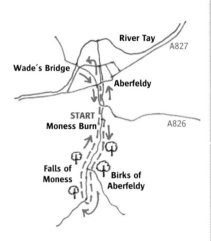

3 miles/5km

Easy, half day walk

An easy walk for all ages and abilities. The path up through the Birks of Aberfeldy can be muddy in places, and keep an eye on young children as there are some steep drops.

Map: OS Landranger, sheet 52.

Start/Parking: Birks of Aberfeldy car park, off the A826 Crieff road, Aberfeldy. GR: NN 855486.

Log on to this walk at:
www.walkscotland.com/route70

Set off into the den from the car park, following a path through Japanese trees. A few yards on the way forks – go left and cross the **Moness Burn**, then continue through the trees, a mix of oak, birch, hazel and ash.

After a gentle start by the river, the way begins to climb, a series of wooden steps and boardwalks gaining height above the narrowing gorge below where the first of the day's dramatic waterfalls tumble down over the well worn rock.

Soon you'll reach pass the seat where ...rns stopped to rest weary legs and ... his famous ditty.

A little further up, the ...oardwalk swings back on itself to reach ...flight of steps. Before you ascend, take a short detour straight on to a viewpoint overlooking one of the waterfalls. The path climbs above the **Moness Falls**, a raging torrent of white water dropping straight over a high cliff.

At the top of the den, the path crosses a bridge immediately above the waterfall. Once over, bear right and descend steadily through the trees, leading back to the car park.

Join the road below the car park and follow it down towards **Aberfeldy**. A short way on, in the wall on the right, a gap leads to a path following the Moness Burn downstream. It passes through a stone arch to reach Bank Street in the heart of the town. Turn left and follow the main thoroughfare west until you reach Mill Street on the right. A little way down this narrow lane is the 19th century Aberfeldy Water Mill. It was restored in 1987 and is open to visitors, providing demonstrations of oatmeal being made in the traditional Scottish way.

Carry on down Mill Street to the bottom and, turn left along Taybridge Terrace. This skirts along the top of Victoria Park and the local golf course, leading to **Wade's Bridge**. Built in 1733, it was part of General Wade's famous road network and was so well built that over 260 years later it still carries traffic over the **River Tay**. Nearby is the Black Watch Memorial, unveiled some years later in 1887.

The last stretch of the walk follows Taybridge Road up past the putting green. At the crossroads at the top, carry straight ahead up Crieff Road to reach the **Birks of Aberfeldy** car park.

Glen Tarken

Named after an Irish saint who spent much of his time roaming the Highlands of Scotland, St Fillans is a charming little hamlet located at the east end of Loch Earn. For centuries it was a welcome staging post for weary travellers and during Victorian times was popular with holidaymakers looking to escape the soot and grime of Edinburgh and Glasgow. It remains as popular today, and is an ideal base for exploring the surrounding countryside.

To the left of the front of the Four Seasons Hotel, a track branches off from the main road, rising past St Fillans Power Station and houses overlooking **Loch Earn**. Further on, it turns sharp right through a hairpin bend, climbing to cross a bridge over the trackbed of the former Comrie, St Fillans & Lochearnhead Railway.

The line opened at the start of the 20th century but closed less than 50 years later on October 1, 1951 and the rails were later lifted. The old platform and buildings at St Fillans Station are

7 miles/11km
Moderate, full day walk
Moderate walk through forest and over open moor. The estate requests that walkers stick to the track during the grouse-shooting season (August 12 to February 15) and dogs must be kept on the lead out with the forest due to sheep grazing.

Map: OS Landranger, sheet 51.

Start/Parking: Four Seasons Hotel, St Fillans. GR: NN 692245. Free parking in roadside laybys on the A85 adjacent to Loch Earn.

Log on to this walk at:
www.walkscotland.com/route71

now part of a caravan park.

Walk up the track, through a gate, and prepare for a steady ascent between the densely packed trees. In due course, the route reaches a junction. Don't take the track on the right but instead carry straight on to emerge from the forest at a gate. This may be locked but there is space in the fence to climb through.

Ahead is an open moor of bracken and heather. The track runs level for a time, turning back on itself to gain height via a wide zig-zag below **Creag Odhar**. Half a mile on from this, it drops to cross the Allt an Fhionn.

The way rises again from the water before flattening out to skirt through a shallow valley, descending to join another track. At this junction, turn left and follow the track down into **Glen Tarken**, passing the entrance to a tunnel, part of the local hydro-electric network of underground pipes.

Lower down, the track fords the Glen Tarken Burn – there are stepping stones to help you over when the burn is at its normal level. If it's in spate, head for a wooden bridge a short hop downstream. On the other side, turn left at the junction just up from the burn and the track continues down the glen

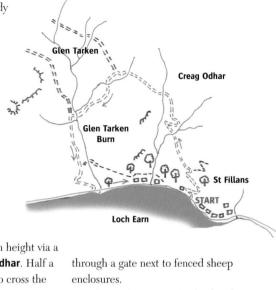

through a gate next to fenced sheep enclosures.

It descends over grazing land with views across Loch Earn, curving right and then left at a pair of stone cottages. Further down, the route crosses the disused railway line again, emerging on to the A85 at a gate by a farm.

Turn left and follow the road east back to **St Fillans**. The grassy verge is wide enough to keep walkers away from the traffic. Pass a small caravan park and yacht club on the right and, beyond this, there are excellent views over the loch. To the west, Ben Vorlich rises to 3231 feet.

Continue along the road back to the start

Moncreiffe Hill

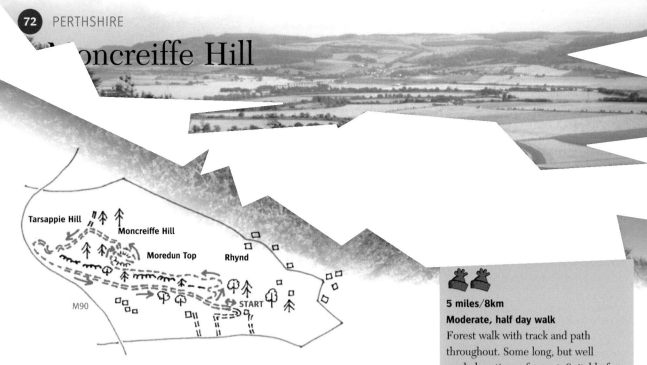

Tarsappie Hill
Moncreiffe Hill
Moredun Top
Rhynd
M90
START

5 miles/8km

Moderate, half day walk
Forest walk with track and path throughout. Some long, but well graded sections of ascent. Suitable for all ages and abilities.

Map: OS Landranger, sheet 58.

Start/Parking: Woodland Trust car park. GR: NO 154193. To reach this follow the A912 out of Bridge of Earn and, immediately on the other side of the bridge over the River Earn, turn right and follow the minor road east under the motorway. A mile and a half on a sign points left up a track to the car park.

Log on to this walk at:
www.walkscotland.com/route72

Moncreiffe Hill, to the south of Perth, is a familiar landmark for anyone heading north on the M90. The motorway nudges the craggy slopes but within the tranquil wooded enclave you could be a million miles from the hustle and bustle of the heavy traffic that is so close by. Walkers are welcome to explore the 333 acres of mixed broadleaf and conifer forest on the south side of the hill, which was bought by the Woodland Trust, a conservation body, in 1988. Subsequent studies have identified over 100 species of plant, animal and bird life to look out for, including red squirrels, green woodpeckers and buzzards.

This route climbs from the base of the hill through the trees to emerge at the highest point where there are panoramic views to savour. Head up to a wooden gate and information board at the top end of the car park. Pass through the gate and a path climbs steadily through the trees to a junction.

Turn right here and the route continues to climb, curving right then left to another junction where a grassy track heads west through the forest.

Don't take this but bear right instead, staying with the main track as it rises through a mix of coniferous trees, oak and sycamore, the grassy forest floor dotted with pink foxgloves.

The track curves left as it gains height and the gradient eases off to run almost level through the trees, emerging at an open viewpoint with vistas south over the River Earn to the Ochils and Lomond Hills.

Bridge of Earn is clearly visible hugging the banks of the meandering River Earn below, while Abernethy can be seen to the south east, its historic tower poking out above the tiny houses.

The path disappears into the trees again, descending slightly before widening into a track to run level along the hillside. Stay with this until you reach an obvious grassy path on the right. This curves up on to the summit of the hill – **Moredun Top**.

From the cairn, a narrow path drops over the west side of the hill to rejoin the ascent path at a junction. Instead of heading back to the original track, turn right and another track descends to a viewpoint with a bench – a short detour.

The track then curves left round the hillside and descends to a wide junction.

Take the right-hand option here and the way drops through mixed woodland, skirting along the edge of an open field, and curves to the left to reach its terminus above a wooden gate.

Carry straight on along a narrow path through the grass to a wooden fence where the way bears left and follows the fence down through the trees and continues on to join a track just above the motorway.

Turn left and the track climbs gently through the trees, eventually reaching the junction at the top of the track from the car park. Retrace your steps down the hill from here.

Glen Lochay

Tucked away beneath a cluster of tall mountains, Glen Lochay is one of Perthshire's most remote and least visited valleys. Far from the crowds, it's the perfect setting for a peaceful, easy leg stretch. The public road through Glen Lochay from Killin ends a short way beyond Kenknock Farm, at a bridge over the Innisraineach Burn. The walk starts here.

Head west across the bridge to a gate. On the far side the track sets out through open land, crossing a large pipeline a short way on. This is part of the extensive local hydro-electric network, much of which is buried under the ground and goes largely unseen. The track follows the **River Lochay** upstream and, a mile on, forks. The left arm drops down to cross the river before climbing to the lonely farm cottage at Lubchurran on the hillside above. It provides access to two Munros – Beinn Cheathaich and Sgiath Chuil. Both can either be tackled from **Glen Lochay** or Glen Dochart, to the south. The glen walk provides a good view to both and may whet your appetite for a future expedition.

Don't take this track today, but go right and the way rises gently, passing a shed before dropping to continue over

grazing land. As you progress there are several small burns – some with bridges – to cross. Thankfully none of those without bridges provide any real obstacle and you should escape dry-shod.

The river below, where these watercourses ultimately end, continues to remain close at hand as the track skirts by a small woodland before crossing the Allt Badour via a more substantial bridge below cottages at **Badour**.

Beyond this is **Batavaime** farm, the last occupied building in Glen Lochay. There are the ruins of cottages higher up the valley, but these have long since been vacated. The track fords the Allt Batavaim and, a short distance on, reaches a junction.

Turn right and follow the track up the slope as it zig-zags steeply before flattening off at the top. Above are the rugged flanks of another Munro, Beinn Heasgarnich, and this is where those heading for its summit leave the track and set off up a narrow path.

To continue this walk turn right and the track leads to a bridge over the Allt Batavaim. There's a gate just before the bridge and, once across, the way strikes east, following a track built to service a pipeline running below ground here.

Although this track runs parallel to the

outward route in the base of the glen, the raised elevation offers a different perspective on the glen and there are some marvellous views to enjoy as you wander east.

The track negotiates a couple more gates before arriving at a concrete bridge over the Innisraineach Burn, located at the top of the pipeline passed earlier in the day. A few yards on the way meets a single-track road. Turn right and follow this down to the start.

7 miles/11km

Moderate, full day walk

Good track walk suitable for all abilities with just a short stretch of steep ascent. The walk runs through cattle and sheep grazing land, so dogs must be on the lead.

Map: OS Landranger, sheet 51.

Start/Parking: End of Glen Lochay public road, a short way beyond Kenknock Farm. GR: NN 465364.

Log on to this walk at: www.walkscotland.com/route73

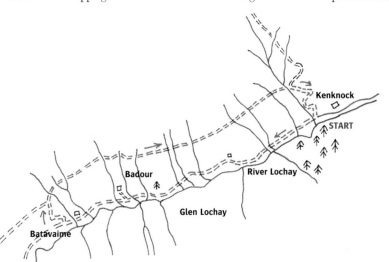

Birnam Hill

A low craggy peak to the south of Dunkeld, Birnam Hill was made famous by William Shakespeare's Scottish play, Macbeth**. The area also attracted the author Beatrix Potter, who spent many holidays here and is said to have drawn the inspiration for some of her famous characters from the Perthshire countryside.**

Set off from the main street through **Birnam** and head up a narrow lane named Birnam Glen to the right of the Beatrix Potter garden. This passes under the A9 and railway and heads left at a red marker post. It climbs to houses and a sign for **Birnam Hill** points left along a surfaced single track road which soon gives way to a track running straight ahead through mixed woodland.

This leads to a private house but, as it curves right towards this, a path breaks off to the left, descending a little over the hillside towards the railway below. It sets a course through woodland of predominantly oak, beech and silver birch, climbing through the trees before dropping towards an open area below old quarry workings on the hillside up to the right. The path meets up with a track from the quarry and this should be followed left down to open ground. Skirt

along the edge of this and pick up a path on the right, signed for Birnam Hill. The way rises again and continues to do so for some distance as it climbs around the south shoulder of the hill. A strenuous pull eventually brings you to the Stair Bridge viewpoint, a very short but worthwhile detour from the main route.

The track continues up through the trees before curving right to level off for a short way below Birnam Hill. A flight of wooden steps and a final short climb lead to the large summit cairn. The top is a fine viewpoint with the hills to the north, including the prominent peak of Schiehallion, visible on a clear day.

To descend, follow the path north down over open hillside and it winds its way through a woodland of Scots pine and larch trees. A slabby viewpoint is the next stop and from here you can look down on the houses of Birnam and, just over the river, **Dunkeld**. The Loch of the Lowes nature reserve – where

ospreys nest – is just beyond.

The way becomes steeper from here and care should be taken as you walk down through the bracken and silver birch trees to meet up with the path coming up from Birnam Glen just above the railway.

4 miles/6.4km
Moderate, half day walk
Short hill walk with good paths but a strenuous ascent and steep descent suitable for fairly fit walkers and older children.

Map: OS Landranger, sheet 52 or 53.

Start/Parking: Beatrix Potter Garden, Birnam. GR: NN 033418. There is a roadside layby just north of the start and car parking is also available at the railway station.

Log on to this walk at:
www.walkscotland.com/route74

Schiehallion

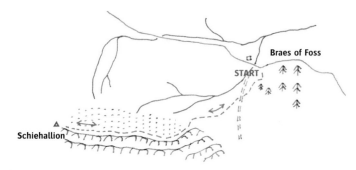

If mountains were motors, Schiehallion would most likely be one of those great big multi-purpose vehicles. Not only does its long backbone resemble the roof profile of such a car, but the peak also carries plenty of passengers. For Schiehallion (1083 metres) is one of Scotland's most popular hills, welcoming thousands of pairs of feet a year. The path to the summit begins in the Braes of Foss car park, located on the minor road between Kinloch Rannoch and the B846 Tummel Bridge to Aberfeldy route.

At the far end of the car park a sign for **Schiehallion** marks the start of the route. It passes through a kissing gate and runs along the edge of a field, with scruffy conifer trees on the left. Higher up, the path goes through a gate and crosses a grassy slope, which can be marshy in places.

Underfoot conditions improve greatly when a good track is joined a little further on. This rises through bracken and heather, crossing a couple of tiny streams as it twists up on to the eastern flank of the mountain.

Sadly the weight of boot traffic tramping up Schiehallion's mighty shoulder has led to some serious erosion problems. Further on, the solid track gives way to peaty ground where evidence of this is all too clear. The eastern part of Schiehallion – including the summit – is owned by the John Muir Trust, which bought the land

through a £300,000 public appeal – £150,000 to buy the mountain and the rest to pay for restoration of the path and on-going conservation work. The trust has also been successful in securing National Lottery money for the project, as well as funding from other sources.

It plans to deal with the erosion of the main path by diverting it south from lower down the mountain, closer to the **Braes of Foss** car park. This will take walkers on to the ridge at a lower point, allowing vegetation to reclaim the existing path.

As the walk progresses, the gradient becomes increasingly steep as the path climbs ever closer to the ridge. Thankfully, when it finally emerges on the crest, the ascent eases off considerably. However, the comfortable peaty base that makes walking such a pleasure gives way to a jagged landscape of quartzite stones and boulders. There is so much rock scattered about up here, that dozens of cairns have been erected over the years, ensuring that route finding is not a problem. Take care to avoid an ankle twist, though, as you head

up the ridge, the top looming into view ahead.

The summit cairn sits on huge slabs of rock which provide an airy platform with views on a clear day east to Loch Tummel on the east and over Loch Rannoch on the west, and Glencoe is visible in the distance.

The return to the Braes of Foss car park is by the route of ascent.

---

6 miles/10km
Challenging, full day walk
A straight-forward mountain ascent with path throughout. Take care on the ridge as the ground is strewn with angular rocks and boulders. This is a good route for those who wish to extend their walking to Munro-bagging. In winter, however, it is a more serious proposition and when the mountain is under snow, this is a route for experienced hillwalkers with crampons and ice-axes and the knowledge to use them.

Maps: OS Landranger, sheet 42 or 52, Harvey's Ben Lawers.

Start/Parking: Forestry Commission Braes of Foss car park. GR: NN 753557.

Log on to this walk at:
www.walkscotland.com/route75

The Murder Hole

The macabre sounding Murder Hole may not seem like the most enticing destination for a peaceful country stroll. Thankfully the spot in question has nothing to do with death, but is rather an author's flight of fantasy. While Galloway does indeed have a Murder Hole linked to a gory legend of abduction and bloodshed it is elsewhere in the county, and not at the western tip of Loch Neldricken where this route leads.

Buchan Hill, a 493 metre high peak.

Pass through a gate higher up and the path soon meets up with the Gairland Burn, taking water from **Loch Neldricken** – the walk's final destination – and **Loch Valley** down to **Loch Trool**.

The route follows the stream up to the western shore of Loch Valley where there's a lovely strip of golden sand, a good place

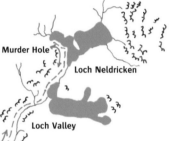

to stop for a break before embarking upon the final stretch of the walk. The loch extends east in the shadow of the evocatively named Rig of Jarkness and at the far end there's a small lochan, Loch Narroch.

Back on the path, continue north past a sheepfold. The way runs parallel with the Mid Burn, a stream linking Loch Neldricken and Loch Valley, to emerge at the southern tip of the loch.

The Murder Hole is a short but rough walk, left around the reedy western shore. It is so called, not because of any dark deeds that happened in this wild and remote spot, but because of a novelist's literary licence. It was created when Samuel Rutherford Crockett penned his book, *The Raiders*. In

5 miles/8km
Easy, short stroll
An easy walk suitable for all ages and abilities, following a good path over grazing land, where dogs will need to go on the lead, and open moor.

Maps: OS Landranger, sheet 77, Harvey's Galloway Hills.

Start/Parking: Bruce's Stone public car park, Glen Trool. GR: NX 415803.

Log on to this walk at: www.walkscotland.com/route76

Galloway there exists the tale of a woman and her son who lived in a lonely cottage on the Bargrennan to Straiton road. The pair were said to welcome weary travellers, but after providing lodgers with a bed for the night they would murder their unsuspecting victims and dump their bodies in a deep, boggy hole on the moor. Crockett took the story, but transported the Murder Hole from Rowantree Junction to Loch Neldricken.

Once you've finished exploring Loch Neldricken, retrace your steps via Loch Valley back to the start.

From the car park, set off east towards Buchan, passing Bruce's Stone, a monument erected in 1929 on the 600th anniversary of the death of King Robert the Bruce to commemorate his victory over an English force in **Glen Trool** in 1307.

Follow the track through a bend, then over the Buchan Burn at the Earl of Galloway's bridge. There's an impressive waterfall on the left here. Beyond the bridge, there's a stile in the fence on your left. Ignore this and continue along the track a little further to another stile, again on the left. Climb over this and a path climbs diagonally across an open field.

A short way up, it passes through a gate in a wall and continues to rise over bracken-covered slopes, accompanied by a stone-built wall on the left. The path skirts round the southern flank of

Stinchar Falls

Choose a good forest walk in Scotland and you'll find much more than just trees. The waymarked route through Carrick Woodlands to the Falls of Stinchar is a fine example. A quiet path leads to an impressive waterfall hidden deep within the heart of the forest. Along the way, pink foxgloves and a profusion of bluebells inject colour into what is one of the largest and most diverse forests in southern Scotland. Ideal for all ages and abilities, the shelter of the trees makes this a walk for that day when the weather is not quite so good.

The starting point for this route is the Forestry Commission car park at **Stinchar Bridge**, on the Straiton to Bargrennan road. From here, follow the access track back down to the road, emerging next to the bridge. Cross over and a path heads west to the right of the burn, passing a signpost for **Stinchar Falls**. The path and burn run parallel through a ride in the dense woodland, crossing several rather springy boardwalks.

Beyond a small dam, the path reaches a wide forest track. Turn left and follow another sign for Stinchar Falls. The track skirts through the trees to emerge above a large felled area where the clearing offers excellent views north and west over woodland and low hills. Further on, the track known as the Aqueduct Road (due to a large underground water pipe running on its north side) reaches a green sign pointing to the falls. A steep path of scattered pine needles descends to a viewpoint above the falls.

They are a modest affair normally but, following a spell of rain, water cascades through a series of small falls linked by a chain of deep pools cut into the rugged rock.

From the viewpoint, a path bears left through the trees and shrubs, widening into a grassy track. Stay on this until a waymarker on the left indicates the start of a short detour into the forest, returning to the track along the riverbank. The path joins the track at a concrete bridge over the River Stinchar. Cross and, beyond a couple of picnic tables below a small waterfall, a path leaves the track on the right and follows the burn through the trees. It arrives at the junction below the dam encountered earlier in the day. Retrace your steps to Stinchar Bridge from here.

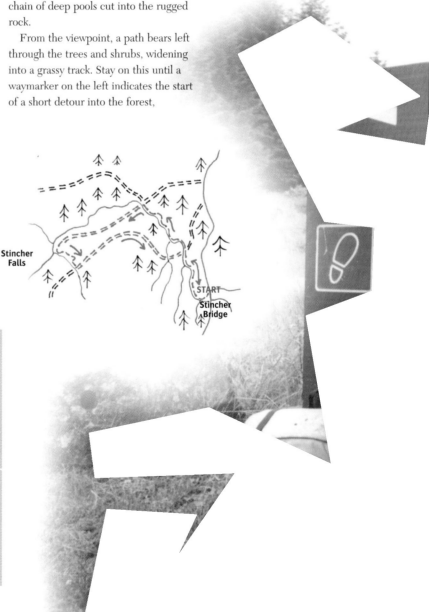

5 miles/8km
Easy, half day walk
Low-level forest walk with path and track throughout. Underfoot conditions can be muddy in places. Suitable for all ages and abilities.

Map: OS Landranger, sheet 77.
Start/Parking: Forestry Commission car park at Stinchar Bridge. GR: NX 395946.

Log on to this walk at:
www.walkscotland.com/route77

Lammermuir Hills

Draped over East Lothian like a patchwork blanket of browns, purples and greens, the Lammermuir Hills offer adventure in a remote landscape of low tops carved up by deep burn gullies. Only a few miles from bustling coastal towns, and the high-speed A1, this lonely wilderness is truly a world away.

The walk starts two miles south of Stenton at a row of orange pan-tiled cottages. Follow the track up to **Stoneypath Farm** and bear right on a track signed to **Johnscleugh**. This climbs to a cottage at Moorcock Hall. Go through a gate and carry straight on, the track rising across grazing land, with a fence on the left. It emerges on to moor at a gate and curves left to another gate higher up.

The way rises through heather, grass and blaeberry bushes and skirts across Mid Hill and to the north of **Clints Dod**. Beyond this flat-topped hill, the track descends to Johnscleugh Farm, reaching a gate behind the buildings. Go through the farmyard and follow a surfaced road down to the valley floor. It makes a sharp right, passes through a gate and joins the main road beyond Whiteadder Water.

Turn left and walk on towards a pylon line. Beyond this the way descends to a ford with a wooden footbridge. Cross a cattle grid beyond the bridge then leave the road, turning left on a track. A flat concrete bridge spans the burn.

A few metres on, climb over a gate and begin a twisting climb. The pylons veer away to the right and at the end of a long, uphill stretch, the track curves sharp right. Leave it and carry straight on along a path through heather, keeping a post and wire fence on your left.

Further on, rejoin the track, turn left and follow it towards forestry. Go through a gate, pass by a corrugated iron shed, and continue on the track to a gate entering the next plantation. Leave the track, turn left, and follow the fence up over heather and grass to a stile and public footpath sign.

Cross the stile and follow a path setting off north-east through a clearing in the trees. This leads to a track but, just before you reach it, there is a narrow burn to cross and a slightly boggy patch of grass to negotiate. The path continues straight on, crossing West Burn before rising through a line of deciduous trees to a metal gate. Continue up the edge of the forest, keeping the fence on your right, to the top corner.

Turn left and walk north-west along the edge of the plantation over **Dunbar Common**. At the end of the trees there is a cluster of wooden gates and a milestone. Cross over and carry straight on along a built-up strip of ground. At the next gate, go straight on and follow an obvious path leading through heather, over the north-east shoulder of **Deuchrie Edge**.

Continue by an abandoned cottage, down to a gate and climb by a stone wall to **Deuchrie Farm**. Join the road and turn left at a junction onto a single-track road leading back to the start.

10 miles/16km
Moderate, full day walk
Obvious track and path over upland moor and low hills. This is a lengthy route suited to fairly fit adults and older children. Two short sections are on quiet country roads where care should be taken.

Map: OS Landranger, sheet 67.

Start/Parking: Cottages below Stoneypath Farm, two miles south of Stenton (three miles south of Dunbar on the B6370). There's space for a handful of cars above the cottages. GR: NT 614713.
Log on to this walk at:
www.walkscotland.com/route78

Pentland Hills

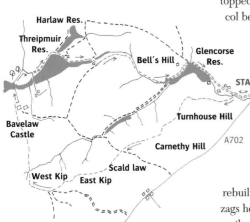

The Pentland Hills are within easy reach of Edinburgh but the rolling open country is far removed from the hustle and bustle of Scotland's capital city. Although low hills by comparison to their sisters in the Highlands, the ascents are nevertheless strenuous. However, excellent views provide ample reward for the ups and downs. Aside from being a regional park enjoyed by walkers, the Pentlands also conceal 13 reservoirs providing Edinburgh and its environs with water. These are home to a variety of birds and wildlife.

Leave the car park and follow the minor road west alongside a small burn. A short way on the road passes a wooden gate on the left. Here a small footbridge spans the burn. Cross, and a path goes through woodland to a stile over a wall. A short stroll over an open field leads to the start of the ascent proper.

The path climbs gorse and bracken covered hillside. There are a couple of stiles to cross as you make your way up to a clump of trees on the first shoulder. Here, the way flattens out briefly with a view down to **Glencorse Reservoir** on your right before rising to the top of **Turnhouse Hill**, marked by a cairn.

Descend to another small cairn-topped summit then drop down into the col between this peak and the next top, **Carnethy Hill**. At the pass, cross a wall and fence at a stile then begin the ascent. The path climbs through heather and grass to the summit of Carnethy Hill.

The descent follows the west shoulder of the hill down into the next col. The path up **Scald Law** has been rebuilt due to erosion and a set of zig-zags helps you gain height quickly and easily.

From Scald Law, the path drops a short distance before splitting. Take the right hand fork down then climb over the pointed tops of **East Kip** and **West Kip**. Follow the dipping track west over open grass and heather. Cross a stone bridge before climbing over the valley to the west of Hare Hill. At the pass there is a gate and right of way sign pointing to 'Balerno'. Follow the track down towards woodland in the distance.

The track skirts the edge of a plantation before entering a strip of beech wood, emerging on to a minor road. Turn right and, at the next junction a short way on, go left, passing through an avenue of tall beech trees.

The road crosses the west end of **Threipmuir Reservoir** and continues to a nature reserve information board. At this point, leave the road and turn right, crossing a stile. Follow a track to the reservoir, along the west shore then across behind the dam at the north end.

At the far end of the embankment, continue round the reservoir to a small dam and stone shed. Cross the dam and, behind the shed, to the left, a narrow path skirts up and round Black Hill. This passes between it and neighbouring **Bell's Hill** then drops to Logan Cottage and Glencorse Reservoir. From here, follow the road clockwise round the loch back to the start.

12 miles/19km
Challenging, full day walk
A long walk with good paths over open hillside. There are some steep ascents. Some sections are on minor roads. This route is best suited to fit adults and teenage children.

Map: OS Landranger, sheet 66.

Start/Parking: Flotterstone Ranger Centre on the A702, three miles south of the A720 Edinburgh city bypass. GR: NT 233632.

Log on to this walk at:
www.walkscotland.com/route79

Cardrona Forest

If walking over remote moor and through peaceful forest appeals to you, then this route in the Scottish Borders is perfect. Cardrona Forest, near Peebles and on the banks of the River Tweed, has a network of paths used by walkers and mountain bikers. This route suits both and to make navigation easy, many of the forest roads have names.

Leave the car park at **Kirkburn** and head along a substantial forest track that follows the Kirk Burn south through the base of the glen. The way runs fairly straight, rising gradually with dense coniferous woodland on the left and open grazing across the stream to the right.

The track reaches a junction. Go left here and climb through the trees on the Glenpeggy Burn Road. The ascent is more strenuous now. Part way up there is a track on the right. Ignore this and carry on until you reach a hairpin bend. Turn left here, on to the Kirkburn Upper Road.

The track skirts on a level gradient round the flank of **Wallace's Hill**, then descends a little before flattening out to reach a junction of tracks. At this point, turn right on the route signed as Castle Knowe South Road and a short climb leads to another fork. Go right here and the way rises through the trees, curving left and then right to emerge from the foliage at a spectacular viewpoint with vistas over the open fields of the Tweed

valley below. From there, follow the track to its end at the edge of the forest.

A path continues straight ahead, running a line between trees on the right and open heather moor to the left. There's a stone wall and wire fence boundary to keep you company. Stay on the forest edge as the path dips before climbing on to **Orchard Rig**. It then descends to the southern-most tip of **Cardrona Forest**.

Turn right here and a path drops quite steeply alongside a fence to the **Highlandshiels Burn**. Cross the tiny stream and on the other side the path rises through bracken to join a track. Turn right and the forest road descends north to a tight hairpin bend where it drops more steeply to the base of the glen. For those on mountain bikes, this is an exciting, fast descent. At the second bend, bear left and follow the track north, rejoining the track to Kirkburn for the final stage of the route.

9 miles/14.5km
Moderate, full day walk
Easy to follow forest tracks and paths on a route suitable for adults and older children, or mountain bikers.

Map: OS Landranger, sheet 73.

Start/Parking: Forestry Commission car park at Kirkburn on B7062. GR: NT 293384.

Log on to this walk at:
www.walkscotland.com/route80

Three Brethren

The enchanting summit of Three Brethren, a low hill near Selkirk, is the high point of this trek over old drove roads once used by Borders cattlemen. The top is dominated by a trio of high stone cairns, the carefully built structures dwarfing the neat white Ordnance Survey trig point. Panoramic views extend over the surrounding countryside, a jigsaw of rolling hills dotted with forestry, grouse moors and sweeping valleys where small towns and villages nestle.

From the telephone box on the **A708** in **Yarrowford**, cross the road and follow a green sign pointing to the **Minchmoor Road**. Walk along a narrow lane past several houses and a playing field and, at the end of the road, a track rises into trees. Further on, another right of way sign directs you up a narrow grassy path and, at the top you join a track and climb through mixed woodland. Ignore a track branching off to the left into the forest and keep going straight up until you reach a gate.

Emerge into a grassy field and the track turns left, running alongside a wall, separating field from forestry. It rises steadily, leaving the field higher up and climbing over open moor.

The Minchmoor Road skirts the flank of **Brown Knowe** to meet the Southern Upland Way (SUW) half a mile west of the summit. At the SUW signpost, turn right and follow the path signed for Yair, over an old drove road on to the top of Brown Knowe, where there is a cairn.

Cross a stile on the summit and descend east along a rounded ridge to the col. Pass over another stile here and the path rises behind a strip of Scots Pine woodland. It climbs over a grassy hillside, dropping to cross a stile in the next dip below **Broomy Law**. Onwards from there the path skirts left round the hill, following a stone wall, to another stile just before a junction of paths above Broadmeadows Youth Hostel.

Don't cross the ladder stile over the wall but carry straight on towards forestry. Pass by a gate on the right – don't go through it but continue left of the wall – and when you reach the trees there's another stile to cross. The track proceeds between the wall and a line of trees on the left. The summit of **Three Brethren** is in view ahead and the way leads straight to the top. Enjoy the view then retrace your steps back to the junction above the youth hostel.

This time, cross the ladder stile and descend south with the wall to your right. It's a fairly steep descent and as height is lost, the path moves away from the wall and runs to the left of the burn. In due course it reaches woodland and continues down the left hand side of this, over sheep grazing land with the ruin of Newark Castle in sight below.

9 miles/14.5km
Challenging, full day walk
Good paths over open hillside. The track up from Yarrowford is a strenuous ascent but once at the top the rest of the route is fairly straightforward. Suitable for fairly fit walkers and older children. Sheep grazing in places along the routes means dogs need to go on the lead.

Map: OS Landranger, sheet 73.

Start/Parking: BT call box in Yarrowford, 4 miles west of Selkirk on the A708. GR: NT 407300. There's a roadside layby at the start with space for several vehicles.

Log on to this walk at:
www.walkscotland.com/route81

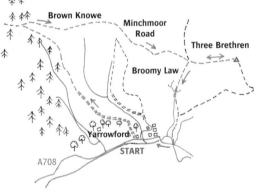

The path emerges on to the A708 at a gate and signpost. Turn right and follow the road west back to the start.

Eildon Hills

The Eildon Hills dominate the landscape of the Tweed Valley. The prominent peaks that rise up above the historic abbey town of Melrose can be seen from miles around and the summits offer panoramas over the gently rolling countryside of the Scottish Borders. Steeped in legend, they are linked with the Romans, King Arthur and the novelist Sir Walter Scott.

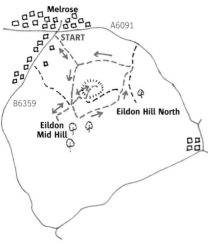

The walk starts at the public car park opposite the entrance to **Melrose** Abbey. Head into the town's market place, continue to the Mercat Cross and then follow the **B6359** road as it heads up and under the bypass.

Once under the main road, keep an eye out to the left for a flight of steps about 20 metres on. These descend through a gap between two houses and there's a sign for 'Eildon Walk' to keep you right.

At the foot of the steps, a path heads uphill, following the edge of fields, to open moor above. There are a couple of stiles to cross along the way and as you climb great views open out over Melrose and the surrounding countryside. It's a good vantage point from which to see the abbey, the last resting place of Robert the Bruce's heart, if legend is to be believed.

The path continues to climb into the pass between the summit of **Eildon Hill North**, on your left, and **Eildon Mid Hill**, on the right. Head for this saddle between the pair where a well-earned breather can be taken before progressing.

The first top to conquer is Eildon Mid Hill. Turn right and a short but strenuous ascent rises on to the summit, the higher of today's two tops. Near to the summit are the remains of a prehistoric burial cairn.

Retrace your steps back to the saddle, then head straight across, following the path on to the top of Eildon Hill North. On the way up, you pass remnants of an Iron Age hill fort over to the right. The peak was also utilised by the Romans who built a signal station here to send messages from a base built in the shadow of the Eildon Hills. All that remains of this early telecommunication hub is a circular ditch running around the summit.

Once you've explored the ancient remains, descend back to the saddle and turn left, following a good path south,

down to the top of mixed woodland. Go left when you reach the trees and follow a track along the edge of the plantation.

In due course, the way forks – take the left branch which climbs gently round the southern slope of Eildon Hill North before descending past Horseshoe Plantation. It continues to lose height, dropping to the top end of a strip of woodland. Follow the edge of the trees down a short way to meet a path on the left.

The path heads north-west, then west hugging the contour of the slope round to rejoin the route of ascent used earlier in the day, at the top of the field. From here, retrace your steps to Melrose.

6 miles/10km
Moderate, half day walk
An energetic climb out of Melrose on to the summits of two low peaks. Track and path throughout. Some sections on the southern side of Eildon Hill North can be muddy after heavy rain.

Maps: OS Landranger, sheet 77, Harvey's St Cuthbert's Way.

Start/Parking: Melrose Abbey. GR: NT 547339. There is parking in the centre of Melrose, opposite the abbey.

Log on to this walk at:
www.walkscotland.com/route82

St Cuthbert's Way

St Cuthbert's Way is a long distance route snaking through Border country from Melrose to Holy Island on the Northumberland coast. It links many historic sites associated with the former Bishop of Lindisfarne and there's a healthy collection of Roman remains along the way. Hearty walkers can trek the entire route in as little as four days but the proximity of towns and villages with good public transport links and fine hotels makes it possible to break it down into a series of less strenuous days out. As a taster, why not try the first section, from Melrose to the pretty hamlet of Maxton?

The tourist information centre next to **Melrose Abbey** is a good starting point for the walk. Before you set off, it's worth popping into the abbey for a taste of the area's religious background. It was built by Cistercian monks in 1136 and, although badly damaged by English attacks during the 14th century, part of the original church still stands.

The way leaves the charming, if chaotic town square and follows the road under the **A6091** Melrose bypass. A short way on, to the left, steps drop down between two houses and a path climbs on to the **Eildon Hills**. It skirts between fields and then rises

between two of the summits

From the pass, the path descends to lush green woodland where tall beech and pine trees throw a leafy canopy over the carpet of bracken and wildflowers. Continue down and the way skirts the bottom of the plantation to emerge at a farm track. Cross and it climbs through a small woodland to reach the peaceful village of **Bowden**.

This is a particularly pretty community where quaint cottages cluster along the tree-lined main street. Go over the main road by the tiny Post Office and a narrow road leads down to a riverside path running east through a delightfully secluded valley. It reaches a farm steading at **Whitelee** and a quiet stretch of country road leads into **Newton St Boswells.**

Put the houses behind you and a real treat awaits – the **River Tweed**. It arrives on the scene as if by accident. The path loses itself in dense shrubbery after passing beneath the busy **A68** and, when you least expect it, hurls you out on to one of the most spectacular viewpoints in the Scottish Borders. A deep blue river vista stretches away below, the Eildon Hills offering the dramatic backdrop for a scene well worth capturing on camera.

The path follows the river for the next stretch and you may be lucky enough to see heron fishing alongside the many ducks. An impressive suspension bridge offers access

10 miles/16km
Moderate, full day walk
Low-level route with path and track throughout suitable for reasonably fit adults and older children. This is a linear route, but there is a good public bus service. Pop into the tourist information centre before you set off – they have timetables.

Maps: OS Landranger, sheets 73 and 74, Harvey's St Cuthbert's Way.

Start/Parking: Tourist information centre next to Melrose Abbey, Melrose. There is parking available in the centre of Melrose.
GR: NT 547342.

Log on to this walk at:
www.walkscotland.com/route83

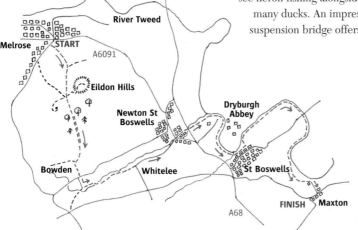

to **Dryburgh Abbey**. Here you'll find the graves of Sir Walter Scott, who died at Abbotsford in 1832, and First World War commander Earl Haig.

The way loops round to the bustling community of **St Boswells** and another peaceful riverside walk, part of which is alongside a golf course, leading to **Maxton** and its unspoiled village kirk and graveyard.

Red Well from Newtonmore

The town of Newtonmore sits in Badenoch, the geographical centre of Scotland. Over-shadowed by the Monadhliath Mountains, walking opportunities abound and every effort is being made locally to encourage this past time. In such remote country, it's easy to spot deer roaming the hillsides, or to surprise Black Grouse nesting in the heather. This route weaves through just such a landscape, skirting by crisp, cool mountain streams and returning through mixed woodland.

From the church, head east along Church Terrace, passing between houses, then go left up a track that narrows into a path, emerging at a children's playpark. Bear right up a paved path to reach Clune Terrace, then turn right and follow the residential street east to a phone box. At this point, go left and follow a single-track road up between open fields, crossing a cattlegrid. Stay with the road as it curves right, then left at a steading.

Follow the road past a derelict cottage and on through **Strone** and when you reach a rundown stone barn on the left, turn left on to a track. This passes through a gate and heads over open moor. Ignore a waymarked path bisecting the track and continue north. Further on, the track fords a stream. Continue past two large cairns to a gate and from here walk north to meet

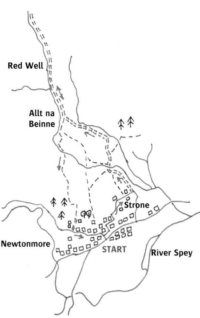

the **Allt na Beinne**. The route bears right here, following the burn upstream, through a narrow glen carpeted in bracken and purple heather. The way starts to climb quite steeply, passing the site of the now demolished Green Bothy. It pulls out of the valley on to open hillside above and, half a kilometre on, reaches the **Red Well**. Down to the left of the track, it sits just above the burn and is easy to spot as the soil around it has been dyed a red-brown colour by the iron in the water.

Turn round here and follow the track back down to the point wher⋯

with the Allt na Beinne. Leave the track as it starts to veer away from the burn. Turn right and cross the stream. A narrow path stays close to the Allt na Feithe Buidhe, following it downstream to a wooden gate. Go through and stay on the track as it bears right, away from the water. In places it is quite wet underfoot, but it soon dries out as a large cairn of quartz is reached. From here, a wide path leads south to a coniferous plantation.

Follow the track along the side of the woodland to an area of recently planted trees blocking the way. Go left and follow the boundary fence east. When you reach the corner, turn right and follow the fence to a stile, which leads into older mixed woodland. A short way on you'll join a track. Turn right and follow this south-west to a cluster of houses on the western edge of **Newtonmore**. The access road takes you down to the public road. Turn left and follow this back to the start.

6 miles/10km
Moderate, half day walk
Track and path throughout. The section heading back towards Newtonmore can be quite marshy. Sheep grazing, so dogs on the lead. Suitable for fairly fit adult and older children.

Map: OS Landranger, sheet 35.

Start/Parking: Public car park next to Church of Scotland, signed off the High Street. GR: NN 715994. Parking is available right in front of the church Monday to Saturday only, or use car park opposite – this is available all the time.

Log on to this walk at:
www.walkscotland.com/route84

The Wildcat Trail

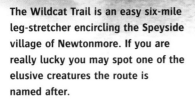

The Wildcat Trail is an easy six-mile leg-stretcher encircling the Speyside village of Newtonmore. If you are really lucky you may spot one of the elusive creatures the route is named after.

From the village square head south-west along Main Street, following the A86 to Calder Bridge. Don't cross, but turn right, following a path along the riverbank. On your left, over the River Calder, are the craggy slopes of Creag Dhubh. The way passes through recently planted native trees including rowan, alder and the rare aspen. Across the water are the ruins of an old mill and lade.

6 miles/10km

Easy, half day walk

A low-level walk for all abilities. Dogs on lead in places (particularly on the higher ground beyond Craggan) due to sheep grazing.

Map: OS Landranger, sheet 35.

Start/Parking: The village square in Newtonmore. GR: NN 714989. There's a free public car park opposite the Church of Scotland, signed off the Main Street.

Log on to this walk at:
www.walkscotland.com/route85

The trail rises to **Milton** where the ruins of an old township can be seen. Approaching Glen Road, you'll pass the remains of two ancient corn-drying kilns. The way continues through Milton Wood, an established plantation of conifers. Follow signs for the Craggan section of the trail, which is reached by turning left up the access road to Upper Knock. The track climbs past three houses and forks at a sign to Craggan. Proceed round the back of the hill past the Craggan sheepfank.

From Craggan there are panoramic views over the town and east towards the mountains of the Cairngorms. Continue across **Strone** moor and the remains of a hut circle where the foundations of primitive Pictish structures can be found.

The path follows the Allt Laraidh down past a series of waterfalls and the ruin of a corn mill and skirts through natural woodlands to join the A96.

Near the remains of the old road bridge there is a grassy path leading to a layby on the road. At the layby, turn right towards **Newtonmore** and follow the path through the woods. It runs south-west, parallel to the road, until you reach a sign pointing left down a side road towards the golf course and **River Spey**. Follow this track across the railway bridge and along the burn until you reach a footbridge over the water.

Do not cross the golf course fairway but follow a signed path to stepping stones leading to the Eilean na Cluanaich.

Walk along the riverbank to the south-west end of the golf course where a signpost points to the village. Don't follow this (unless you want to cut the walk short) continue along the trail as it follows the river upstream

Approaching the junction of the Spey and River Calder there are views again of Creag Dhubh and Glen Truim. The trail passes under the railway line and a short way on arrives at **Spey Bridge**, built on the orders of the Duke of Gordon in 1765. Cross the road and the trail runs along the east bank of the River Calder to reach Calder Bridge. Turn right here and follow the A86 road back into Newtonmore.

Three Laggan Munros

Anyone who has watched the BBC's Sunday evening drama Monarch of the Glen **will have had a sneak preview of the beautiful countryside around Loch Laggan. Much of the series was shot in this part of the world, the big house at Ardverikie on the wooded shores of the loch being one of the main locations.**

Set off from the car park, cross the concrete bridge over the River Spean and follow the track up towards the farm steading at Luiblea. At the first junction you reach, bear left away from the property and the track rises gently along a low embankment above the Abhainn Ghuilbinn. It climbs more steeply to a

14 miles/22km

Challenging, full day walk

Upland walk with track and path for the majority of the route. Suitable for fit, experienced hillwalkers and teenage children. Choose a good clear day and make sure you go prepared with waterproofs, food and drink. In winter it is a more serious proposition and when the mountains are under snow, this is a route for experienced hillwalkers with crampons and ice-axes and the knowledge to use them.

Map: OS Landranger, sheet 42.

Start/Parking: Large layby on A86 at track junction to Luiblea.
GR: NN 433830.

Log on to this walk at:
www.walkscotland.com/route86

gate and another junction.

Turn right here and the route continues to climb, skirting round the south west flank of Binnein Shuas, the craggy peak up to your left, to reach a three-way junction above a small lochan. Go left here and the track runs fairly level, before dipping to a wide wooden bridge over the Allt Coire Pitridh at the south west end of **Lochan na h-Earba**. Follow the track along above the loch until it turns sharp left and a path branches off on the right. Take this. An obvious stalker's path rises over the hillside, following the Allt Coire Pitridh upstream. As with many stalker's paths, the route is quite well graded, but it can still be a hard slog. As the path nears the col, it reaches a junction.

Branch off to the left here on a path heading north, into the col between **Creag Pitridh** (924 metres) on the left and **Geal Charn** (1049 metres) on the right. It's up to you which of the two peaks you want to do first. For Geal Charn, head up to the left, a fairly obvious path rising up the south flank to reach the summit. Retrace your steps to the col and then head over a low dip before climbing up on to Creag Pitridh. It's a shorter ascent than its neighbour, but the final haul is a bit steeper as the path negotiates a route up through the crags to the summit where you'll be rewarded with fine views north over

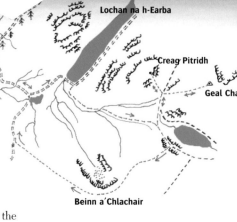

Loch na h-Earba towards Loch Laggan. From here, retrace your steps to the stalker's path junction.

Follow the path south up the flank of **Beinn a'Chlachair** (1087 metres). The route wends its way through rocks before flattening out and climbing more gently towards the summit. As you get nearer, the path skirts round the back of crags dropping into breathtaking Coire Mor Chlachair on the right. The top has a large stone cairn.

Head west away from the summit and descend in a north-westerly direction over the broad slope of the hill. It is fairly steep and trekking poles come into their element here, taking some of the pressure off weary knees. Underfoot is a carpet of heather and grass and it can be wet in places, particularly lower down where the slope flattens off before rising gently to reach a track. Follow this north for a mile to reach the three-way junction above the small lochan. Turn left here and retrace your steps back to the start.

Loch an Eilein

This is a delightful lochside stroll through ancient Caledonian Pine Forest, in the shadow of the Cairngorm mountains. Keep your eyes peeled because you never know what you'll spot when you venture into the forests of Rothiemurchus, near Aviemore. The trees are home to red and roe deer, red squirrels, the rare pine marten and the even rarer wildcat.

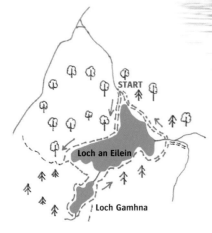

Centuries ago the Scottish Highlands were carpeted in woodland like this but over the years the trees have been used for timber to build homes and to power industry and only pockets of the original ancient Caledonian Pine Forest remain. One of the finest examples is here at Rothiemurchus in Speyside.

Lurking amid the gnarled old trees is **Loch an Eilein** – Loch of the Island – and there's a path all the way round. As you peer out over the water, you won't fail to spot the island from which the loch takes its name. It sits about 50 metres off the west shore and is home to a fourteenth century castle said to have been the home of Alexander Stewart, illegitimate son of Robert II of Scotland. Known as the Wolf of Badenoch, he was, among other things, responsible for burning down Elgin Cathedral.

Leave the car park at its south end and a path leads to public toilets and a little visitor centre. It then heads on to a pleasant beach at the northern tip of the loch, which enjoys an uninterrupted view over the water to Clach Mhic Cailein. Turn right here and the path leads along the west side of the loch.

The path skirts round the western tip of the loch and reaches a junction. Ignore the grassy path on your right and continue along the main route. It briefly touches the shoreline again before rising gently through trees.

At the next junction, turn right, leaving the main path, and a slightly narrower route heads south, skirting round **Loch Gamhna**, a body of water about a third of the size of its neighbour. Much of this section of the walk is through open country, which makes a fine contrast to the more heavily wooded environs of Loch an Eilean.

The path rejoins the main loch circuit next to a bridge spanning the outflow from Loch Gamhna. Turn right and the path re-enters pine forest. It briefly skirts by the loch before twisting off into the forest, finally turning north for the return leg.

At the next junction, where a track joins from the right, carry straight on across a small footbridge and the way widens. It sits some way back from the loch, but you can still see the water through the trees.

In due course the track reaches a gate. Go through and follow a wall down to the water's edge where a narrow path runs along the shore. This rejoins the track just before it crosses a wooden bridge over the loch's outflow.

Carry on to reach the visitor centre and retrace your steps from here back to the car park.

5 miles/8km

Easy, half day walk
Low-level woodland path throughout suitable for all ages and abilities. It can be wet and muddy in places.

Maps: OS Landranger, sheet 36, Harvey's Cairngorm.

Start/Parking: Rothiemurchus Loch an Eilein car park (there's a charge). GR: NH 897085.

Log on to this walk at:
www.walkscotland.com/route87

Meall a'Bhuachaille

The Glenmore Forest Park in the shadow of the Cairngorms is one of the most popular parts of Scotland, frequented by walkers, skiers and watersports enthusiasts. Meall a'Bhuachaille sits on the northern edge of this stunning scenic area and the summit is an ideal spot to cast your eyes over the surrounding countryside.

To the left of the forest shop at the back of the car park, a green waymarker indicates the start of a grassy track through the forest, rising steadily towards a junction a short distance on. Here, turn left and continue to climb as the sandy track gains height through the dense coniferous forest, a narrow burn taking its course down to the left. A kilometre from the start the way swings left to cross the burn on a substantial wooden bridge. It runs level for a few yards before turning right to climb again, the verges lined with heather, grass and blaeberry bushes.

After a strenuous climb, the path emerges on to open moor at the top of the trees. The summit of **Meall a'Bhuachaille**, glimpsed briefly through gaps on the way up through the forest, can now be seen clearly, standing proudly ahead. Continue to climb, a wide path cutting a route through the

heather over peaty ground.

The path rises on to a broad ridge to the west of the summit where another path crosses at right angles. Turn right and following it up on to Meall a'Bhuachaille. The route of ascent is dotted with cairns and the top itself boasts a large cairn and stone shelter. From there, descend east over an obvious path that loses height gradually to begin with. Several hundred yards beyond the summit, a path branches off to the right. Take either route as they join up again before the path drops more steeply behind **Ryvoan** bothy. Take care as the path can be muddy on the steep section and there are loose stones underfoot.

At Ryvoan bothy, the path meets up with a track. Turn right at this small stone structure and follow the track to a junction of rights of way with green signs pointing back towards Nethy Bridge and Braemar. Carry straight on here, the track dropping gently through a narrow steep sided glen, the slopes above dotted with Scots Pine

trees and great falls of rock and scree. At **An Lochan Uaine** there is a small stretch of water surrounded by trees and, on one side, a scree slope. The track runs round above the west shore and a path branches off to the right. Don't take this but stay with the track, following it down towards Glenmore Lodge.

Further down from the lochan the track forks. Take the right hand arm, cross the Allt na Feith Duibhe by a bridge next to a **Glenmore** forest sign and emerge on to a minor road at Glenmore Lodge. Follow the road behind the sprawling complex and continue past Norwegian Lodge to a reindeer farm park at the bottom. Leave the road here and a stretch of pavement leads back to the start.

6 miles/10km
Challenging, full day walk
Good path up through forestry and over open moorland, returning on forestry track and minor road. With a strenuous climb early on, this route is suited to fairly fit walkers and older children.

Maps: OS Landranger, sheet 36, Harvey's Cairngorm

Start/Parking: Glenmore forest shop and visitor centre. GR: NH 977098. This is located five miles from Aviemore on the road to the Cairngorms, the turn off on the left just beyond the entrance to the Glenmore campsite on the right. There is a charge for the car park.

Log on to this walk at:
www.walkscotland.com/route88

Map labels: Meall a'Bhuachaille, Ryvoan, An Lochan Uaine, START, Loch Morlich, Glenmore Forest

Loch Garten

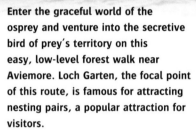

Enter the graceful world of the osprey and venture into the secretive bird of prey's territory on this easy, low-level forest walk near Aviemore. Loch Garten, the focal point of this route, is famous for attracting nesting pairs, a popular attraction for visitors.

Each spring, fresh from their African winter break, ospreys nest in the extensive pine woodlands and bring up their young. Efforts to increase numbers of this all too rare creature have been extremely successful here and the RSPB has established a fascinating visitor centre above the tree-lined loch. It gives bird lovers outstanding sights of the ospreys as they go about their business and, in addition to informative displays, a television link provides live pictures from a nearby nest so you can watch all the activity without disturbing the birds.

Set off south from the car park, following an obvious track towards the loch. The way skirts beside the water offering tempting glimpses through the native Scots Pine trees, over the rippling blue surface to the low hills beyond. Ignore a track on the right 500 metres from the start and continue south, and you'll soon head away from **Loch Garten** into the trees.

START

Loch Garten

A970

Loch Mallachie

5 miles/8km

Easy, half day walk

A low-level route following well graded forest tracks and paths. If you want to see the ospreys, the best time to go is between April and August.

Map: OS Landranger, sheet 36.

Start/Parking: Woodland car park one mile south of B970 on Loch Garten road - follow signs for RSPB Ospreys. GR: NH 973185.

Log on to this walk at:
www.walkscotland.com/route89

The way curves gently right to reach **Loch Mallachie**. Follow the track along the north shore of the loch as it swings right to reach a junction. Turn left and a path skirts along the top of Loch Mallachie, a tiny square of water bounded on three sides by trees. Around 200 metres from the junction, the path goes right, away from the water, and heads north through the tall pines.

At the next junction, carry straight on and stay with the path until you reach a crossroads. Turn right and follow the track north, rising gently over a low mound before descending to another junction. Turn left here and the track curves down, passing under a line of electricity pylons, to reach a small car park adjacent to the **B970** at its junction with the Boat of Garten road.

Head for an information board at the top of the car park and pick up a path, running north-east, parallel to the road. The way swings right in due course and leaves the B970. It continues to skirt along the edge of the forest, this time close by the minor road leading down to Loch Garten, to reach a junction where a forest track crosses your path. Cross the track and continue south along the path as it undulates gently to reach the car park just over a kilometre on.

Ben Venue

If you're interested in ticking off tops, but aren't quite ready for the heights of Munro-bagging, consider Ben Venue. This craggy peak in the heart of the Trossachs takes its rightful place on the list of Grahams, a table of Scottish Hills between 2000 and 2499 feet high.

Set off from the Forestry Commission car park at the west end of **Loch Achray**. Walk south along the **A821** road for around 400 metres to the entrance to the **Loch Achray Hotel**. Turn right, following a wooden signpost for **Ben Venue**, and head up the drive towards the hotel. Follow the way round the building and, behind it, join a forest track that crosses a burn and heads west, staying close to the Achray Water.

A short way on, you'll reach a fork in the track. Bear left here and follow the track to a crossroad a little further on. Go straight on, climbing through the trees, the track narrowing into a path. There are some fairly muddy sections during this part of the ascent but stepping-stones can be found over some of the dampest patches.

Higher up you'll join another track. Cross over and continue up the track on the other side as the way climbs through Gleann Riabhach. When this ends, a path leads to the top of the plantation, emerging on to open hillside. The route bears north at this point, climbing under the crags of Ben Venue

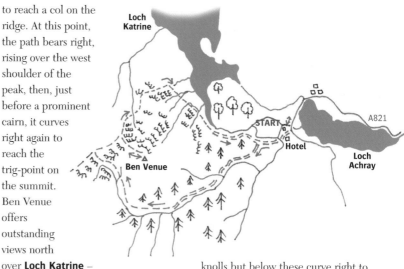

to reach a col on the ridge. At this point, the path bears right, rising over the west shoulder of the peak, then, just before a prominent cairn, it curves right again to reach the trig-point on the summit. Ben Venue offers outstanding views north over **Loch Katrine** – Glasgow's water supply – and the Trossachs, and east across Achray Forest and Loch Venachar.

There are two options for your return. The most straightforward is to follow the route of ascent back down to the car park. Alternatively, to create a circuit, return to the prominent cairn on the ridge below the summit and, at this point, bear right and head down into the gully below. This route needs careful navigation and caution should be taken when descending the slope. Cross the stream lower down and continue to descend, contouring round the ridge towards a line of fence posts coming down from the right.

You will have to bear left away from the posts to walk under some rocky

knolls but below these curve right to head east to reach the top of a gully where the route descends alongside the fence line towards Loch Katrine. As the steep gradient begins to ease, pick up a path on the right that leads back to the forest. Within the trees a good track leads back to the hotel. Retrace your steps from here to the car park.

🥾🥾🥾

6 miles/10km
Challenging, full day walk
An energetic climb through forestry and over open hillside best suited to reasonably experienced hillwalkers and older children. Paths in the trees can be wet and muddy. Returning by the route of ascent is the easiest option, but walkers who are confident of their navigational skills over open hillside can make a circuit of the route.

Maps: OS Landranger, sheet 57, Harvey's Ben Ledi

Start/Parking: Forestry Commission Achray public car park. GR: NN 505068.

Log on to this walk at:
www.walkscotland.com/route90

Ben A'an

Ben A'an is one of the most prominent landmarks in the Trossachs. At 461 metres high, it is by no means a lofty peak, but its craggy slopes give it the mountainous air of a much taller hill. The ascent is arduous, rising straight up from the shores of Loch Achray through dense commercial forestry. The reward, however, comes in the form of panoramic views as far as the Pentland Hills, near Edinburgh, and the Arrochar Alps, above Loch Long.

From the car park, cross the **A821** and, on the other side, the start of the path to the top of **Ben A'an** is well signed. It climbs steeply through dense larch trees, following the Allt Inneir upstream.

About half a kilometre up, a viewpoint on the left, signed from the path, offers a short detour and provides a welcome breather. The rocky summit of the peak can be spied through the trees from here.

The gradient eases and, as you approach the edge of the forest, the top dominates the view ahead. Free of the trees, there are vistas to neighbouring Ben Venue and west over the blue ribbon of Loch Katrine.

From the edge of the plantation, the path climbs steeply again, rising over a slope of grass and heather moor. It follows a burn into a col to the east of the summit and curves round to the north of the peak. It's not far to the top now. A final stiff but thankfully short pull brings you out on the high point, a magnificent elevation from which to savour the delights of the Trossachs, the heavily wooded slopes of this stunning area of upland country rolling out below you.

On a clear day you should be able to see west to the Arrochar Alps, where the craggy Cobbler lurks, and north to the Southern Highlands where Ben More and Stob Binnein are among the most easily recognised. You can measure just how far you've climbed by looking south to **Loch Achray** below, where the walk began.

Ben A'an was originally known as Am Binnein (the rocky peak), but in his writings the famous novelist Sir Walter Scott decided to replace the old Gaelic name and it has stuck ever since.

To finish the walk, retrace your steps back down the hill to the car park, taking particular care over some of the loose terrain below the summit.

2 miles/3.2km
Moderate, half day walk
A short, but steep ascent of a low top, suitable for fit adults and older children. Take care on loose ground near the summit.

Maps: OS Landranger, sheet 57, Harvey's Ben Ledi.

Start/Parking: Forest Enterprise Ben A'an car park on the A821, next to Loch Achray. GR: 509071.

Log on to this walk at:
www.walkscotland.com/route91

The Bonnie Banks of Loch Lomond

There's a well-known song about the 'bonnie, bonnie banks of Loch Lomond' which has made Scotland's largest area of fresh water famous throughout the world. Stretching from Balloch, north of Glasgow, to Ardlui, the loch is surrounded by high mountains, with dense woodland carpeting the slopes as they sweep down to the water's edge. The West Highland Way skirts the eastern shore, and the section below Ben Lomond, the most southerly Munro, forms part of this fine circuit.

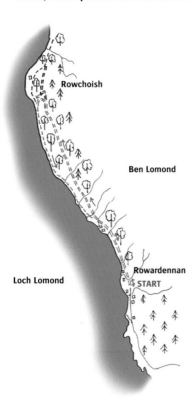

The walk strikes out on a good forest track, returning through woods by the water, where it is possible to discover roe deer or wild goats grazing silently among the trees. This countryside forms part of the 75,000 acre Queen Elizabeth Forest Park, managed by the Forestry Commission, and walkers are welcome to discover its charms.

Set off from the information board within the car park and head north along the single-track road to **Rowardennan** youth hostel. The path splits at the hostel gate and the walk continues to the right, passing a metal gate and following a West Highland Way marker.

After a few metres, the track forks again. Take the left and cross a small stream, before skirting along behind the hostel. The path passes a cottage and a new house on the right and bears left to cross a burn before heading through mixed woodland, bramble and bracken.

Cross the next junction and the track passes a stone shed, then crosses a cattlegrid and runs along the shore of **Loch Lomond** to Ptarmigan Lodge. At the entrance to the lodge, bear right and the track climbs to a metal gate. From here, it rises through silver birch, beech, oak and rowan and curves up past a narrow waterfall, cutting a tight course down a deep crack in the rocks. The ascent continues for some distance until you reach the high point, from where it's downhill all the way to the next junction. At the lowest point of the track, an obvious grassy path branches off to the left, curving down through woodland to the lochside, emerging at a beach with views across the water to Tarbet. At the top of the beach, the track meets a path. Follow this south into the trees

and go quietly, for you may be lucky enough to spot roe or red deer.

The path undulates gently along the bank of the loch and if you're out after it's been raining take care on rocks and tree roots as they can be slippery.

Continue south and, beyond a bridge made of railway sleepers, there's a fine pebble beach that makes an ideal lunch spot with fine views down Loch Lomond.

Carry on until you reach a wooden footbridge. Once across this, the path bears left up a narrow flight of makeshift steps rising through bracken to rejoin the track above Ptarmigan Lodge. From here, retrace your steps to the start.

7.5 miles/12km
Easy, full day walk
Sheltered track and path through woodland and along lochside, suitable for walkers of all ages and abilities.

Maps: OS Landranger, sheet 56, Harvey's West Highland Way.

Start/Parking: Public car park at Rowardennan pier. GR: NS 360986. There are public toilets here.

Log on to this walk at:
www.walkscotland.com/route92

Bracklinn Falls

If you are ever in Callander, be sure to head for the Bracklinn Falls. Located in the woods above the town, the spectacular tumble of white water has been impressing visitors since the Victorians flocked here in the nineteenth century.

At the back of the car park, a small path descends to an information board where the route proper begins. Turn left and a good solid path runs east through mixed woodland. It skirts the edge of a tall plantation of conifers on the right, scrubland covering the hillside to your left, before emerging on to open hillside, with views over the valley of the River Teith.

The path rises gently along the edge of an open field before descending wooden steps where the rumbling of the falls becomes ever louder, confirming your approach. Popular with visitors as far back as the Victorian era, the falls come alive as the **Keltie Water** squeezes through narrow rock channels. There's a little bridge over the most impressive bit and, on the far side, a natural platform of rock offers a good spot from which to view the frothing turbulence below.

From here, a path climbs through the trees. It follows the river east, perched high above the channel below to your right. The woodland narrows and open

fields soon appear on the left. Continue along the path as it curves right, emerging into a grassy field where sheep are often to be found grazing. Bear left at this point and walk up the field to a fence at the top. Follow this to the right to reach a shed at the end of a track and turn left, heading up the track.

The route climbs round the open hillside and enters forestry. Carry on up through the trees and, at the next junction of tracks, head left and descend to a bridge over the river. The way rises to meet a road on the other side.

Turn left and follow the road south. You can follow this back to the car park at the start, or add an extra challenge to the route by climbing **Callander Crag**.

Where the road kinks and skirts woodland, look out for a sign on the right for the crag. It is the wrong way round for this approach and can easily be missed.

A narrow path climbs through the trees on to open hillside. After a stiff ascent, it arrives at a stone monument marking the summit. This elevated spot offers views over **Callander** and the

surrounding countryside.

Walk straight on over the top and the path descends into forestry to a small wooden footbridge in a dip. Turn left here and a decaying set of over 300 wooden steps descends through the trees. Watch your footing, especially after rain. The way eventually joins a track far below. Turn left, then left again when you reach the public road and walk back up to the car park.

4 miles/6.5km
Easy, half day walk
Easy walk through woodland and over open country with a short but strenuous ascent to the top of Callander Crag (optional). No dogs. Suitable for adults and older children.

Maps: OS Landranger, sheet 57, Harvey's Ben Ledi.

Start/Parking: Bracklinn Falls car park. This is a short drive out of town, up a steep narrow road that leaves the A84 opposite the Roman Camp Hotel. GR: NN 637083.

Log on to this walk at:
www.walkscotland.com/route93

Beinn an t-Sidhein

You can't go far in the Trossachs without stumbling upon reference to the area's legendary hero, Rob Roy Macgregor. A famous reiver and retriever, he stole cattle from the wealthy landowners and distributed the proceeds to the poor. If the hills and woodlands of the Trossachs could speak, they'd doubtless have many a tale to tell about his exploits.

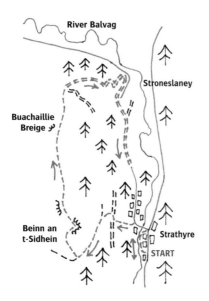

Born into the warring Clan Gregor in 1671, Rob Roy swapped life as a simple farmer for an altogether more exciting career battling the nobility who threatened to crush his way of life. Rallying his men, Rob Roy raided the fertile Carse of Stirling, plundering cattle. Although he was caught three times, he always managed to escape. After a turbulent career, he died in 1734 and is buried with his wife Mary and two of his four sons at the tiny kirk in Balquhidder. His legend, however, lived on and has inspired many, including writers and film makers.

Rob Roy's grave is just a stone's throw from **Beinn an t-Sidhein** and there is every chance he scaled this peak at least

once. Today's walker has the luxury of a waymarked path but the spectacular views from the summit remain little changed.

Leave the car park by its entrance, turn left and follow the A84 road north through **Strathyre**. Pass by the village shop and a bus stop and then turn left on a minor road opposite the Munro Hotel. This crosses the **River Balvag** by an old stone bridge. Carry on to a T-junction ahead. Turn left here and, a few metres on, there's a signed forest walk path on the right. Follow the blue marker posts as the way rises quite steeply up the hillside, passing through dense coniferous Strathyre Forest.

The path emerges on to a forest track. Turn right and a short way on there's another waymarker on the other side. Leave the forest road here and follow the path back into the trees and up the hill. Not far on, you reach another track. Again, following the blue marker, turn left here and continue up, remaining with the main path and ignoring smaller paths branching off on each side. Stay with the blue waymarkers and the route finally leaves the woods and rises on to open hillside.

When the path forks, take the right. It climbs over the southern flank of Beinn

an t-Sidhein to reach the top. Continue north along the path over a couple of humps to **Buachaille Breige**, a craggy outcrop at the end of the broad ridge. Descend north, bearing right towards the edge of the forest until you reach an easy-to-see break in the trees. Within the trees, pick up a forest track and continue your descent until you join the public road just south of **Stroneslaney**. Turn right and follow the road south.

The road cuts through tall woodlands of pine and there are some lovely tranquil strips hemmed in by moss-covered stone walls. In due course, it arrives at the T-junction. Retrace steps through Strathyre to the car park.

---

6 miles/10km
Challenging, full day walk
Forest path and track with waymarkers and open hillside suitable for all fairly fit walkers and older children.

Map: OS Landranger, sheet 57.

Start/Parking: Public car park at south end of Strathyre. GR: NN 560167.

Log on to this walk at:
www.walkscotland.com/route94

Kirkton Glen

The tiny church in the picturesque hamlet of Balquhidder is at the centre of an increasingly popular Scottish pilgrimage. The famous outlaw Rob Roy Macgregor is buried here and each year thousands of visitors seek out his final resting place, many spurred on by the Hollywood movie starring Liam Neeson and Jessica Lange.

Rob Roy died in Balquhidder in 1734 after a lifetime spent roaming the mountains and glens of the southern Highlands.

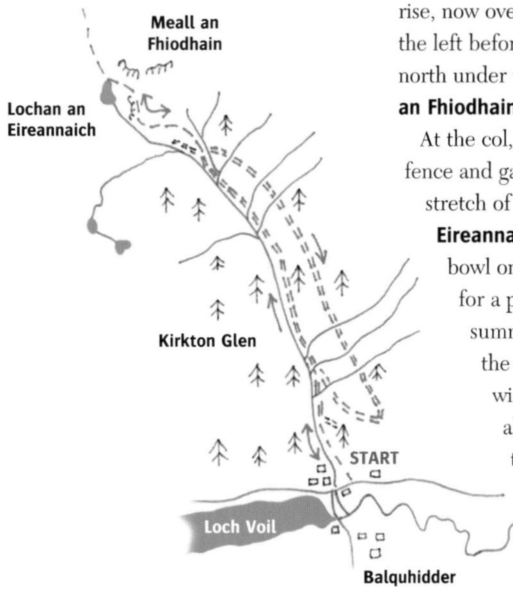

The church, where Rob Roy now lies, alongside his wife Mary and two of their four sons, is the starting point for a walk up **Kirkton Glen** to a remote lochan in the col at the top. The grave sits in the shadow of the ruined original kirk just a few metres from its replacement and is well worth a visit before you set off.

A narrow path heads off from the back of the churchyard and runs through trees towards a waterfall. Just before it reaches this, signs for the footpath point right. Follow these to a stile over a fence then continue up a track ahead. This climbs to the left of a large green metal box and continues to rise steeply through the trees to a fenced enclosure, part of the public water supply. A short way on you'll reach a crossroads.

Several wide tracks converge here.

Carry straight on, up Kirkton Glen, keeping a burn in the dip of the valley to your left. The track rises, but at a more gentle rate. As it gains height, the way disappears into the trees again before emerging just short of the top of the forest.

The track forks with the left hand arm continuing north and the right one curving east. Ignore both and instead take a narrow path straight ahead signed to 'Glen Dochart'. This climbs over a felled stretch of ground to a fence at the top of the forest. The path continues to rise, now over grassy hillside. It curves to the left before heading east and then north under the craggy towers of **Meall an Fhiodhain**.

At the col, the way arrives at a metal fence and gate. To the left a small stretch of water, **Lochan an Eireannaich**, nestles in a shallow bowl on the hillside. This is ideal for a paddle or swim on a hot summer day but watch out for the odd metal can or length of wire on the bottom. You may also spot shoals of fish or tadpoles, depending on the time of year. From the lochan retrace steps to the forest track.

Back on the track, turn left and follow the way as it rises before flattening off to run along the hillside, through tall trees then an area of younger conifers. There are excellent views down the glen and over **Loch Voil**. The track runs level for two miles before curving right and dropping to the crossroads. From there, retrace steps to the start.

6 miles/10km

Moderate, half day walk

Forest track and path throughout. A fairly strenuous ascent through Kirkton Glen, suitable for reasonably fit walkers and older children. There are sheep grazing on higher ground above the plantation so dogs on lead out with the forest.

Map: OS Landranger, sheet 51.

Start/Parking: Balquhidder Church. GR: NN 536209. There's a small public car park next to the church.

Log on to this walk at: www.walkscotland.com/route95

Map labels: Meall an Fhiodhain, Lochan an Eireannaich, Kirkton Glen, START, Loch Voil, Balquhidder

Glen Ogle Rail Trail

The old Callander and Oban railway line closed to traffic as far as the lonely staging post of Crianlarich in 1965 after a rockfall in Glen Ogle. While trains still ply the route between there and the west coast terminus, the trackbed over the section that fell victim to the avalanche of stone has been transformed into an enjoyable walk suitable for all the family, with the return journey following a good path in the base of the glen.

There's a useful information board at the start. From here, cross the busy **A85** and head up the track towards the Scout Station. This is the former **Lochearnhead** station building, subsequently restored and converted

into an outdoor activity centre for young people. Although marked private, the Scouts do welcome visitors, so if you want to see the old station, there should be no problem.

The trail doesn't actually pass by the building and a few metres from the main road there's a path on the right with a small sign marking the way. Follow this up the hillside, a steep little climb leading to the line of the railway. In places, the ascent through bracken can be muddy underfoot, but as height is gained great views over **Loch Earn** reward the effort.

A yellow arrow on a post marks the start of the trackbed section of the walk. It climbs steadily over a good, even gradient. The ground underfoot has recently been upgraded to ensure it is

suitable for cyclists as this section of the walk forms part of a long distance cycle network.

Two miles on, the walk crosses the impressive stone structure of **Glen Ogle** viaduct, another fine viewpoint. Continue up the line until a stile on your right marks the high point of the route and the start of the way down. Cross the stile and follow an obvious path down the glen. This gradually descends over open ground to meet the burn in the valley floor before rising to cross the A85.

A wooden ladder stile spans the fence at the side of the road. Be very careful crossing as traffic is fast, especially downhill, and visibility is not great in either direction. Once safely over, the path leads over a tussocky stretch of ground. After two further stiles and a river crossing, the way crosses sheep grazing land. Here the path is a little less distinct but there are frequent waymarkers to keep you on course. As Lochearnhead nears, the path passes through small patches of woodland, crosses a burn and arrives at a kissing gate. It emerges on to a track and, a short distance on, you are back at the start.

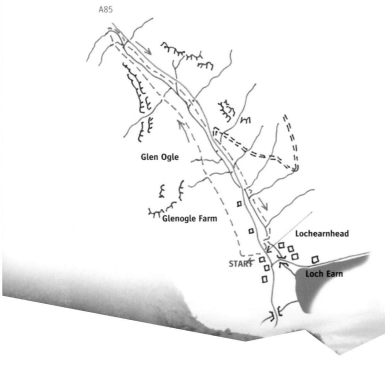

5 miles/8km
Easy, half day walk
Easy walk on low level path and well made former railway trackbed suitable for all ages and abilities.

Map: OS Landranger, sheet 51.

Start/Parking: Information board on the A85 on northern edge of Lochearnhead. GR: NN 587240. There is a public car park in centre of Lochearnhead.

Log on to this walk at:
www.walkscotland.com/route96

Railway Ramble from Killin

Two old railway trackbeds combine with more recent forestry tracks to give walkers a high level taste of Glen Dochart. The route follows the old Killin branch railway up out of the village of Killin, before switching to the trackbed of the former Callander and Oban railway as it rises through the trees to the head of Glen Ogle. Both routes closed to rail traffic in the autumn of 1965 and, with the tracks gone, the routes of the old railways are ideal terrain for walkers and mountain bikers. The network of tracks through the forest is a more recent addition to the landscape and walkers are positively encouraged to make the most of it.

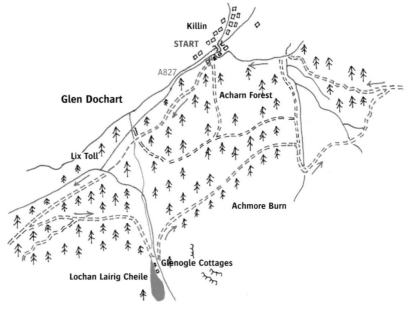

Start at the bridge over the Falls of Dochart and head out of **Killin** on the **A827**. At the end of a row of cottages on the left a track strikes off to the left. It skirts in front of two large houses to reach a high gate. Go through and bear right immediately, following the track under a bridge. From here, the line rises very gently under the canopy of leafy trees.

Two kilometres on – beyond Acharn Farm – the line is crossed by a forest track. Carry straight on, following a narrow path into woodland beyond a gate. It can be a bit overgrown here but very shortly the path widens back out and, in due course, emerges on to the A85 at **Lix Toll**.

Cross the road with care and pick up a track on the other side. This continues to rise at the same gentle gradient to reach the site of the former Killin Junction Station where an old platform and ruined station cottages lurk in the undergrowth.

As you approach the junction another old railway trackbed comes down on the left to meet the route. Turn back on to this where the two meet and follow it east as it rises through forestry, curving gently right. You may spot deer here if you go quietly.

The track climbs and curves right to **Glenogle Cottages** at the northern end of **Lochan Lairig Cheile**. Recent tree felling means there are views to Loch Tay to enjoy. Just before the houses, a narrow path goes left, taking you to the main road. Cross and walk up to a car park and picnic area where the Crannog snack van does a great burger.

Follow a track through the picnic area to a high gate, pass through and continue along the track as it skirts round the hillside through forestry, enjoying panoramas over **Glen Dochart**, Killin and Loch Tay.

The track reaches a T-junction. Turn right and climb up to a bridge over the **Achmore Burn**. The ascent is short but steep. Cross the stream and stay on the track to reach a tall transmitter where you leave the forest plantation at a high gate. At the next junction, turn left and a surfaced track passes through a gate and descends steeply through forestry to meet up with the public road at the bottom. Turn left and follow this for the last leg into Killin.

13 miles/20km

Challenging, full day walk

A long walk for fairly fit adults and older children, with solid tracks underfoot and a final short section along a quiet country road. The route is suitable for mountain bikes.

Map: OS Landranger, sheet 51.

Start/Parking: Falls of Dochart, Killin. GR: NN 573325. There is a well signed free public car park to the north of the falls.

Log on to this walk at:
www.walkscotland.com/route97

Beinn Lora

Rising from the shores of Ardmucknish Bay, Beinn Lora offers what are arguably some of the best views in the west of Scotland. Tall conifers, interspersed with leafy patches of oak, birch and rowan, carpet the hill's northern slopes. The summit, however, stands out from the pines, providing panoramas as a reward for a strenuous ascent from sea level.

A path begins in the Forestry Commission's Lora Forest car park, located on the southern edge of the village of **Benderloch**. Follow it into the trees and carry straight on, avoiding a turn off leading up the hill to the right. Let blue waymarkers guide you as the path climbs gently at first. It curves up to the right and the walking becomes ever more demanding as the gradient increases. A bench at the top of the steepest section provides a welcome resting point and an excellent view north over Loch Linnhe to Kingairloch and Morvern.

The path flattens out slightly here but continues to rise through a break in the trees to another viewpoint where it meets up with a path descending into the forest. Carry on making your way up, following the blue posts. The route climbs steeply once again and continues to ascend until it reaches the edge of the forest. Just before this, however, there is

a chance to visit the **Eagles' Eyrie** viewpoint, signed off the path and well worth the short detour.

Back on the main route, the way emerges from the forest on to open moor. There is a picnic table here and a kissing gate in the high deer fence through which you must pass. Again there are more cracking views, this time down the Firth of Lorne towards Oban. An obvious trail strikes out over the heather. Initially it descends a little before climbing on to craggy **Beinn Lora**. Conditions underfoot are inclined to be a touch marshy on this stretch.

When you arrive at the top a short distance on, you'll find a trig point and, on a clear day, more wonderful views. To

the north, beyond the sprawling forest, is Loch Creran and, to the south, you should be able to see the yachts moored at Dunstaffnage Bay marina. Over to the west are Ben Cruachan and Loch Awe.

Make your way south from the trig point to the edge of the summit and Connel and its cantilever bridge, spanning the Falls of Lora and once conveyance for both road and railway, come into view.

When you're ready to head for home, return to the forest by the same path and follow it down. When you reach the bench encountered early in the walk, turn left and the way loops back to the car park.

3 miles/5km
Easy, short stroll
A short but strenuous forest and moorland walk over good paths. For fairly fit adults and older children.

Map: OS Landranger, sheet 49.

Start/Parking: Lora Forest Walks car park (next to fuel station), Benderloch. GR: NM 905378.

Log on to this walk at:
www.walkscotland.com/route98

The Cobbler

8 miles/13km

Challenging, full day walk

While the main summit ridge of The Cobbler is easily attainable, the south and centre tops are very exposed, require scrambling and a good head for heights. The south top in particular can, and should, be avoided unless you are competent at climbing and accompanied by an accomplice for safety. In winter it is a more serious proposition and when the mountains are under snow, this is a route for experienced hillwalkers with crampons and ice-axes and the knowledge to use them.

Maps: OS Landranger, sheet 56, Harvey's Arrochar Alps.

Start/Parking: Ardgartan on the A83 just north west of the campsite. GR: NN 271036.

Log on to this walk at:
www.walkscotland.com/route99

The 884-metre high Cobbler, or Ben Arthur, is one of Scotland's most easily identifiable peaks. The lumpy, jagged summit ridge throws down such a gauntlet that thousands of people huff and puff up its slopes every year. This route shuns the traditional ascent from Succoth, starting instead at Ardgartan, a little further down the shore of Loch Long, convenient for those staying on the campsite or at the youth hostel.

From **Ardgarten**, follow a gravel path from the campsite along the riverbank towards the visitor centre (marked on the OS map as an information point). About 500 metres along this path, cross the **A83** trunk road at a point where two white wooden poles mark the start of the climb. The muddy path strikes up the hillside, gently at first, then more steeply as you brush past an evergreen plantation before crossing a broad forestry track. Clamber up the steep grassy slopes in a northerly direction to reach an obvious shoulder that tops out at around 550 metres, giving an excellent view down **Loch Long**, said to the deepest body of water in Scotland and is used for harbouring naval submarines.

Head north-west along a path towards the fearsome-looking south top of **The Cobbler**. The path winds its way below this before climbing to the main middle summit where a test of nerve is required to conquer its zenith. Approaching the strange bouldery spire from the north, you have to thread yourself through a rock window known as Argyll's Eyeglass before clambering up onto the top boulder. This, however, is a challenge only for competent scramblers with a head for heights and is not recommended for novices.

To the north-east, the neighbouring Munro of **Beinn Narnain** now draws the walker on. Walk on to the third of the Cobbler's tops, then drop down into the col below, where there's a small lochan.

The ascent of Narnain is straightforward enough even if the paths come and go as you pass through small boulder fields. Steep slopes rise to the stony summit, where a cairn, then a stone-built trig point mark the top, above a climbers' crag known as Spearhead Buttress.

From here, retrace your steps back down to the col between Beinn Narnain and the Cobbler, bear left at the tiny lochan and walk down the glen, following the Allt a'Bhalachain towards the giant Narnain Boulders. Continue down, crossing the stream at a weir, to reach the top edge of forestry.

The path drops through the trees to meet a track. Don't continue ahead on the path, but turn right and follow the track as it contours round the slope to eventually rejoin the path up from Ardgartan, used at the start of the day.

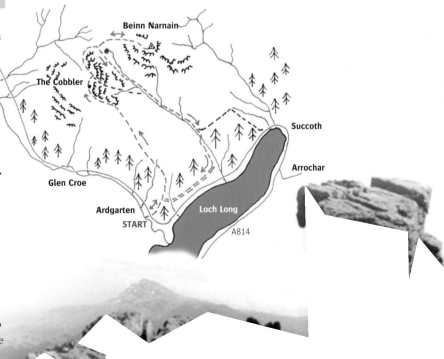

Search for the Superfortress

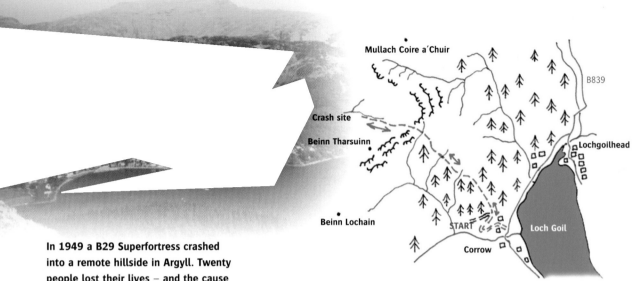

Mullach Coire a'Chuir

B839

Crash site

Beinn Tharsuinn

Lochgoilhead

Beinn Lochain

START

Loch Goil

Corrow

In 1949 a B29 Superfortress crashed into a remote hillside in Argyll. Twenty people lost their lives – and the cause of the accident remains a mystery. A memorial now stands on the spot where the plane went down, surrounded by a fair scattering of wreckage. It is the destination for this rough and ready trek.

The adventure begins at **Corrow Farm** and riding stables, a mile west of **Lochgoilhead**. From a gate at the back of the yard, a track zig-zags up to the foot of a firebreak in dense coniferous forest. This ride is the only way through the trees and it's a steep ascent. The way leads past an aerial and continues to a metal gate half-way up the break. The ascent does not let up until the top of the plantation, below craggy outcrops.

From here, skirt left, following the edge of the forest in a north-west direction. There are a couple of ankle-twistingly steep burn channels to negotiate before the top corner of the plantation is reached. At this point, head due north up the slope towards the col between Stob na Boine Druim-fhinn and **Beinn Tharsuinn** (it's easy enough to identify on the map as there's a 508m spot height marked just east of the bealach on the OS Landranger series).

From the col, walk down the glen

towards a fence at the top of a fairly new area of forestry. There's no path, but stay in the base of the valley and you should not go wrong. When you reach the fence, bear left up, out of the bottom of the glen and keep your eyes peeled to the right for the first signs of wreckage. The main area of wreckage, which is easily spotted from the fence, covers a piece of ground about the size of a tennis court. At the top of it all, a stone cairn has been built as a memorial to the 20 men who died when the B29 Superfortress came down on this lonely piece of hillside in January 1949. The crash site grid reference is NN 161022. Developed by Boeing, the Superfortress was described as a 'very heavy bomber'. Work on the project began late in 1939 and the first one made its initial flight on September 21, 1942. However the American Airforce had ordered the plane into quantity production months before this first flight. The plane's features included pressurised crew compartments, a central fire-control system and remotely controlled gun turrets.

Remains of the four mighty Wright R-3350-57 Cyclons 18-cylinder air

cooled radial engines, which developed 2200hp each, are still to be found along with large sections of fuselage, wing and hydraulic wheel units.

From the crash site, retrace steps back to Lochgoilhead.

5 miles/8km
Challenging, full day walk
A short but arduous walk over rough terrain with no real path and a steep ascent at the start. This is an adventure suited to adults and teenage children who don't mind straying from the beaten track. Dogs on lead due to sheep grazing.

Map: OS Landranger, sheet 56.

Start/Parking: Corrow Farm, near Lochgoilhead. There's space to park on a wide grassy roadside verge just south of the start of the track leading into Corrow Farm. GR: NN 186004.

Log on to this walk at:
www.walkscotland.com/route100